Kaplan Books Relating to College/University Admissions

Guide to College Selection

Newsweek/Kaplan College Catalog

Graduate School Admissions Adviser

Kaplan Books Relating to Admission Tests

SAT

SAT Math Workbook

SAT Verbal Workbook

ACT

GMAT

GMAT Verbal Workbook

GRE

GRE Verbal Workbook

GRE and GMAT Math Workbook

LSAT

NCLEX-RN

TOEFL CBT Exam

TOEFL Exam Workbook

Essential Review for the TOEIC Exam

Kaplan Basic Skills Books

Grammar Power

Math Power

Word Power

Writing Power

Guide to Studying in the USA

Edited by
Marilyn J. Rymniak, Patty Mac Kinnon,
and the Staff of Kaplan, Inc.

Simon & Schuster

NEW YORK · LONDON · SINGAPORE · SYDNEY · TORONTO

Kaplan Publishing
Published by Simon & Schuster
1230 Avenue of the Americas
New York, NY 10020

For bulk sales to schools, colleges, and universities, please contact the Order Department, Simon & Schuster, 100 Front Street, Riverside, NJ 08075. Phone (800) 223-2336. Fax (800) 943-9831.

The sidebar in chapter 9 on proverbs is from *Developing Cultural Awareness* by Robert L. Kohls. Reprinted with permission of Intercultural Press, Inc., Yarmouth, ME. Copyright © 1994.

Special thanks are extended to Linda Volpano, Patty Mac Kinnon, Courtney Watson, Tom Kleinert, Tony McCormac, Mara Del Margo, and Pedro Salazar.

Editor: Ruth Baygell
Contributing Editors: Jose Flores, Leigh-Ellen Louie, Rochelle Rothstein
Cover Design: Cheung Tai
Interior Page Design and Layout: David Chipps
Production Editor: Maude Spekes
Editorial Coordinator: Déa Alessandro
Executive Editor: Del Franz

Manufactured in the United States of America

October 2001

10 9 8 7 6 5 4 3 2 1

ISBN: 0-7432-1425-0

Table of Contents

About the Authors

Carl DeAngelis is Assistant Director for Fulbright and Academic Services at the English and Special Services division of the Institute for International Education (IIE). DeAngelis is also the editor of English Language and Orientation Programs in U.S. (ELOPUS), the definitive catalog of ESL programs published by IIE and used as reference worldwide.

Ed Devlin is President of Pacific Coast Educational Services, an independent consultancy and an Internet-based advisory and university selection service. Devlin has edited numerous publications for NAFSA: Association of International Educators and has directed, taught, and otherwise been involved with ESL and other international programs for the past 30 years.

Lorin Gold was recently Director of Global Leadership Programs at Metro International, where she directs both the International Student Leadership Network and Global Classroom. Gold has worked extensively in the labor unions of New York City, teaching a large range of subjects from ESL to preparation for college.

Alyssa S. Goldberg was recently ESL Communication Specialist for International Programs at Kaplan, Inc. Goldberg received a Master of Arts degree in Communications from the University of Wisconsin and has taught ESL at the university Level and in IEPs for a number of years.

Carol Hirsch served as project co-editor of this book. Until recently, she was International Program Associate at Kaplan. Hirsch was also a teacher and curriculum writer at Kaplan and is currently Senior Editor at Moody's Investors Service.

Nancy Katz was recently Director of the Midwest Office and Corporate Relations of World Education Services. With over 16 years of experience in international admissions and foreign credentials evaluations, Katz has been actively involved in presentations and committees of both AACRAO and NAFSA.

Sal Longarino directed New York University's Office for International Students and Scholars from 1989–1997, and was Chair of NAFSA's Region X (New York and New Jersey) in 1995-96. Longarino is currently serving on the Board of Directors of Metro International, a nonprofit organization in New York City that serves international students and scholars in the New York metropolitan area.

Patty Mac Kinnon is Director of International Academics at Kaplan. She has over 14 years of experience in research and curriculum development, teaching, testing, and program management in both the academic and corporate environments. Patty has been an active member of and presenter at both NAFSA: Association of International Educators and TESOL.

Marilyn J. Rymniak was until recently the Executive Director of International Programs at Kaplan, Inc. For 25 years, Rymniak has been a foreign language/ESL specialist and a leader in the international education field, holding national and regional positions with NAFSA: Association of International Educators and TESOL.

K. Aaron Smith is Associate Director for International Programs at Kaplan. A theoretical linguist and classical language enthusiast, he has taught TOEFL Prep and ESL for many years and has developed second language curricula for university-bound international students.

Tracy Snyder is Associate Executive Director for Metro International, where she develops and implements cultural enrichment programs for international students and scholars. Snyder has worked with international student populations at Harvard University, Boston University, Lesley College, and the University of Nebraska.

A Special Note About Kaplan International Programs

So you have decided to study in the United States for a university degree. How much do you already know about the system of higher education in this country? How well have you planned your course of study?

No matter how well you can answer these two questions, there is much that you can learn about the American system of higher education before you begin your studies: You should plan very well before getting on a plane. Studying in this country is very expensive and involves a huge commitment and sacrifice on the part of you and your whole family. You owe it to yourself to be as prepared as possible before making a final decision on where and how you will pursue your studies.

This book is designed to help you prepare for and plan your course of study in the United States. It will guide you through every phase of the process: understanding the American system, selecting a major, choosing a school, obtaining a student visa, succeeding on campus, and even returning home and finding a job. If you're certain that you want to do all of these things, you need the expert advice and practical information contained on these pages.

About 500,000 international students pursued academic degrees at the master's or doctorate level at universities in the United States in 1999–2000, according to the Institute of International Education's Open Doors report. This trend of pursuing higher education in the United States, particularly at the graduate level, is expected to continue well into this century. Business, management, engineering, and the physical and life sciences are particularly popular majors for students from other countries. International students are also taking advantage of opportunities for research grants, teaching assistantships, and practical training or work experience.

If, after you complete this book, you would like additional help and information, you may be interested in Kaplan's International Programs. These programs were created to assist international students and professionals who wish to enter the United States university system. The programs are designed for students who have received most of their primary and secondary education outside the United States in a language other than English.

For more information, or to apply for admission to any of these programs, contact us at:

Kaplan International Programs
370 Seventh Avenue, Suite 306
New York, NY 10001 USA
Telephone: (917) 339-7591
Fax: (917) 339-7505
Website: http://www.kaplaninternational.com

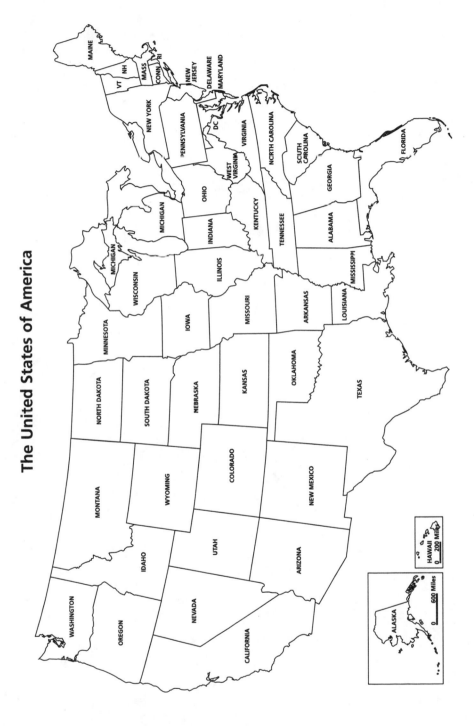

The United States of America

Higher Education in the United States

University of Georgia

Higher Education in the United States

1

Americans place no age limit on what they call "going to college." Though the traditional college age is 18–24, you are likely to see 35- and 50-year-olds—and even 70-year olds—studying alongside you in colleges and universities. The concept of life-long learning is a unique part of the system of higher education in the United States. More than 15 million Americans attended college on a full-time basis last year.

What else is unique about the American system of higher education, and what makes it so popular? To sum it all up in five words: variety, diversity, flexibility, accessibility, and choice.

The phrase *freedom to choose* sums up perfectly how Americans expect their educational system to operate. Our network of colleges and universities doesn't offer a "one size fits all" philosophy. In fact, the American system is one of the only educational systems in the world that does not have a central Ministry of Education that dictates standards for curriculum and admission throughout the country.

Unfortunately, this diversity can make choosing a school in the United States more difficult for an international student. So why do so many international students come to this country for postsecondary study each year?
- There are over 3,300 accredited postsecondary schools in the United States, with more than 600 major fields of study.
- American universities are located in some of the world's largest cities, as well as in small, peaceful, rural farm communities and in safe, suburban areas.

- American universities are extremely diverse, ranging from small, liberal arts colleges with 300 students to large "multiversities" with over 50,000 students.

- Gaining entrance to universities in the United States can be easier than gaining entrance to public universities in many other countries, since those might have limited space and very difficult entrance exams.

- American universities impose no age limits. The concept of lifelong learning pervades the United States education system, which means that you can begin your education at any age.

- American universities offer comprehensive education programs, from the practical associate degree to the prestigious doctorate. You can get anything from vocational training to a postdoctoral degree.

Career training in the United States has many possibilities. You could complete any of the following plans:

Length of Time	Type of Course
3–6 months	A short course in a specialized vocational area Example: computer data entry
1 year	A certificate-level course with a specific focus Example: graphic design
2 years	An associate degree course in a technical field at the technician level (Many of these degrees are transferable to 4-year degree programs.) Example: computer systems analysis
4 years	A bachelor degree program in one of many academic fields.
2–7 years	A graduate or professional-level degree

HOW DO YOU COMPARE?

If you want to know how you compare to the more than 500,000 international students currently studying in this country, here are some facts taken from the Institute for International Education's *Open Doors Report* 1999–2000, a statistical report on international students in the United States:

Sources of Funding

The most common sources of funding that international students use for their studies in the United States are:

Personal and family finances	67.9%
U.S. college and university funds	18.0%
Home government or home university funds	5.9%
Home country private sponsor	2.5%
Current employer	2.3%
Private sponsor in the United States	2.3%

Where Students Come From

Students from many countries studied in the United States last year. Here are the top 12 countries:

1. China	54,466 students
2. Japan	46,872 students
3. India	42,337 students
4. Republic of Korea	41,191 students
5. Taiwan	29,234 students
6. Canada	23,544 students
7. Indonesia	11,300 students
8. Thailand	10,983 students
9. Mexico	10,607 students
10. Turkey	10,100 students
11. Germany	9,800 students
12. Malaysia	9,074 students

Most Popular U.S. Schools

1. New York University	New York, New York
2. University of Southern California	Los Angeles, California
3. Columbia University	New York, New York
4. University of Wisconsin at Madison	Madison, Wisconsin
5. Purdue University	West Lafayette, Indiana
6. Boston University	Boston, Massachusetts
7. University of Michigan	Ann Arbor, Michigan
8. University of Texas	Austin, Texas
9. Ohio State University	Columbus, Ohio
10. University of Illinois	Urbana, Illinois
11. Harvard University	Cambridge, Massachusetts

Did you know the following facts?

1. In the first two years of an undergraduate program, it is very likely that an engineering student will take general education courses such as English composition, history, math, and language in order to fulfill university requirements.

2. With online courses, it is possible to obtain a degree from a post-secondary institute without ever having to sit in a classroom.

3. Students with low grade-point averages and low standardized test scores can still be admitted to postsecondary schools. Many community colleges and undergraduate institutions have open admission and accept all who apply.

4. A student can earn a bachelor's degree, a master's degree and a doctorate degree in three different majors. For example, a student might get a B.A. in government and law, an M.A. in history, and a Ph.D. in political science.

5. International students make up a very small part of the student body at most U.S. universities. In fact, most universities will have fewer than 4% international students.

Most Popular U.S. Locations

International students tend to prefer large cities over rural areas.

1. Los Angeles, California
2. New York, New York
3. Chicago, Illinois
4. Boston, Massachusetts

Most Popular Majors (Fields of Study)

1. Business and Management
2. Engineering
3. Math and Computer Sciences
4. Other (General Studies, Communications, Law)
5. Social Sciences

6. Fine and Applied Arts
7. Health Professions
8. Intensive English Language
9. Humanities
10. Education
11. Agriculture

SCHOOL ACCREDITATION AND RANKING

What is the "best" school of engineering in the United States? Is it Princeton or Penn State? MIT or Carnegie Mellon? What is the best school for international studies? Tufts? Georgetown?

The United States does not have a centralized governmental Department or Ministry of Education to make sure that educational institutions uphold the highest standards of quality. Instead, the American system relies on volunteer groups of educators and professionals to ensure that schools provide the best programs through a process called *accreditation*. Accreditation makes sure that minimum standards are being met but does not rank institutions according to the quality of their standards. Of the 5,000 or so postsecondary institutions in the United States, only 3,300 are accredited.

With so many educational institutions to choose from, and no central Ministry of Education to rely on, it is difficult to determine which schools are "best." The diversity of education here makes it possible for students to choose their own "best" school. It is important to find a school that is appropriate for you. Regardless of the prestigious name of the institution, if it doesn't fit your needs, it is not the best school for you. Most published rankings of institutions are subjective; there is constant debate when these rankings are published because no one ever agrees on the fairness of the method for establishing the rankings. Rankings are probably more important at the graduate school level than at the undergraduate level.

There are two types of educational accreditation: institutional and specialized. An *institutional* accrediting agency evaluates an entire institution in terms of its mission and the agency's standards. It accredits (that is, it approves or recognizes) the institution as a whole. Institutional accreditation is provided by regional associations of schools and colleges (each named after the region in which it operates (Middle States, New England, North Central, Northwest, Southern, Western). The websites for these accrediting associations are:

1. **Middle States Association of Colleges and Schools**
   http://www.msache.org

2. **New England Association of Schools and Colleges**
   http://www.neasc.org/cihe/cihe.htm

3. **North Central Association of Colleges and Schools**
   http://www.ncahigherlearningcommission.org

4. **Northwest Association of Schools and Colleges**
   http://www.cocnasc.org/

5. **Southern Association of Colleges and Schools**
   http://www.sacscoc.org

6. **Western Association of Colleges and Schools**
   http://www.wascweb.org/senior/list.html

A *specialized* accrediting body evaluates particular units or programs within an institution. Specialized accreditation, also called *program* accreditation, is often associated with national professional associations, such as those for engineering, medicine, law, or teacher education.

Accreditation is based on:
- *Rigorous institutional self-study*
- *Onsite visits by educational peers*
- *Submission of an official report*

Accrediting associations make sure that institutions have appropriate, stated educational objectives; have financial resources to meet those objectives; can support the objectives over a period of time; and ethically advertise the objectives to prospective students.

Look for the accreditation affiliation for the college or university of your choice. It will usually be displayed on the college brochure or catalogue. Going to an accredited school is important because:

- As an international student, it is the only way to know that an institution is recognized in the United States and by your home government.
- Credits can be transferred only among accredited institutions.
- Scholarships, fellowships, grants, and other financial and prestigious awards for study are given only to accredited institutions.

Though we strongly recommend that you check out the accreditation status of the schools you are considering, do not waste a lot of time trying to find published rankings of universities. Rather, try to find the school that is best for what you want to study.

PLANNING THE ADMISSIONS PROCESS

Americans are said to be obsessed with time. We do, in some ways, consider it a valuable commodity. Just look at the way we speak of time in English:

We save time.
We spend time.
We waste time.
We kill time.
We find time.
We lose time.
We create time.

Time management is considered an important skill in American life. It is essential that you begin to practice time management now in preparing to study in the United States. Establishing a good plan ahead of time will save you a lot of money and worry later on. In fact, making a plan will help you save time!

Three years is the ideal amount of time to spend planning for study in the United States. Most students don't plan this far in advance, however, and it is likely that you will have one or two years to plan. If this is true for you, you still need to take all of the actions listed below but in a more compressed period of time.

If your current proficiency level of English is fairly low, or if you are just beginning to learn about the U.S. system of higher education, try to begin your preparation as soon as possible.

Most schools in this country operate on a September-to-June academic calendar, so the timetable begins in September. Admission can also occur in January in some cases.

The basic requirements for admission to educational institutions in the United States are:
* *A strong academic background*
* *Adequate financial resources*
* *A good command of the English language*

THE SURE-BET TIMETABLE

I want to start my studies in the United States in September of _____

Two or Three Years Before Admission Target Date

1. Make an initial assessment of your academic goals.

Your school transcripts will be critical in your admission to an American school, and it is crucial that you have a strong academic background. Are you getting higher than average scores on your comprehensive tests? For undergraduate studies, most U.S. schools require 12 years of education with the appropriate high school diploma or secondary school certificate. For graduate studies, most schools require a prerequisite degree, or at least the equivalent of a baccalaureate degree.

2. Make an initial assessment of your English skills.

Take the TOEFL Exam (Test of English as a Foreign Language) as early as possible to find out your level of English. This will give you an idea of how much more English you need to learn before you can study for a U.S. degree. You can schedule an appointment to take the test, so it will be easy to get an immediate assessment of your English level.

Most American universities require the following minimum TOEFL scores for admission. The more competitive the school, the more likely it will require a higher score. Many community colleges will accept slightly lower scores.

    TOEFL Paper-Based Test: 550–610 points
    TOEFL Computer-Based Test (CBT): 213–253 points

The Educational Testing Service (ETS), the creator of the TOEFL, estimates that an average student can increase his or her TOEFL score 40 points for every 300 hours of intensive English study. So if you recently scored a 400, you have a lot of studying to do before you have an admissible score to an American university.

TOEFL Basics

The TOEFL is designed to test your ability to understand standard North American English. It is written and administered by the Educational Testing Service (ETS), a private, not-for-profit company based in Princeton, New Jersey. The TOEFL was developed to help American and Canadian colleges and universities evaluate the level of English language proficiency of the international students they want to admit.

The TOEFL is offered as a computer-based test in most areas of the world, taken at a testing center, by yourself, at a time you schedule. A few countries such as China continue to use the paper-based TOEFL. The major difference between the computer-based test and the paper-based test is that the computer-based TOEFL includes a required essay.

Registering
Telephone (609) 771-7100
Fax: (609) 771-7500
Email: toefl@ets.org
Website: http://www.toefl.org

Scoring
There is no pass-fail score for the test. Each school decides its own policy on acceptable scores. When you take the computer-based test, you will be able to know your score immediately before leaving the test center. Official score reports will be mailed 4-5 weeks later. The total score for the computer-based TOEFL is reported on a 40–300 scale. For the paper-based TOEFL, scores range from 310–677.

Test Day Tips
- Arrive at the test center at least 30 minutes before your scheduled test time. If you arrive late, you may not be able to take the test at that time and your registration fee will not be refunded.
- Bring proper photo identification with you such as your passport. Also, don't forget you appointment confirmation number, which is given to you when you register for the exam.
- Bring a list of schools and addresses to which you would like your test scores sent. You can have scores automatically sent to four schools at no cost.

3. Enroll in an English language program in your country.

When assessing an English language program, look for the following features:

- A program that has trained teachers who are native speakers of American English
- A program that emphasizes real communication skills, as well as grammar
- A program that emphasizes academic English
- A program that uses TOEFL to measure your progress
- A program that is recognized in the United States

You may also want to consider spending some time in the United States during your school vacation studying in an Intensive English Program. You can use that time to learn about schools you may want to attend in two years.

4. Get information about additional American entrance exams you may need to take.

Most universities require applicants to take one or more academic entrance exams, in addition to the TOEFL. There are usually no passing or failing grades on these exams, but your score will have an effect on the overall competitiveness of your application.

If you think you might be interested in become a teaching or research assistant, you might need to take the TSE (Test of Spoken English). The TSE is test that measures the ability of nonnative speakers of English to communicate orally in English. The test is delivered with audio-recording equipment.

Here are the website links to some of the tests you might have to take.

For English language:
  TOEFL/TSE
  http://www.toefl.org

For undergraduate admissions:
  SAT (Scholastic Aptitude Test)
  http://www.collegeboard.com
  (Note: The SAT I: Reasoning Test is the most widely used test, though you might be asked to take an additional SAT II: Subject Test as well.)

For graduate and professional admissions:

> **GRE** (Graduate Record Exam)
> http://www.gre.org
> for liberal arts, science, math

> **GMAT** (Graduate Management Admission Test)
> http://www.gmat.org
> for business school

> **LSAT** (Law School Admission Test)
> http://www.lsac.org
> for law school

> **MCAT** (Medical College Admissions Test)
> http://www.aamc.org/students/mcat
> for medical school

> **DAT** (Dental Admission Test)
> http://www.ada.org/prof/ed/testing/dat.asp
> for dental school

You don't need to register for these exams until one year before your admission date, but you should become familiar with their formats, where they are offered in your country, and how and when scores are reported.

Computer-based testing is now required for some of these admissions tests in many countries. Check the websites for specifics. Do not be concerned if you have little or no computer experience: These tests are easy to take, and before taking the official test, you will be given time to practice getting comfortable with the computer.

5. Begin to identify the colleges to which you would like to apply.

Check around your city for information about colleges and universities in the United States. Talk to others who have studied in the United States. Write for applications and information on scholarships and fellowships, and ask for school catalogues. Refer to the resource list at the back of this book to get you started.

6. Check on the State Department's student visa requirements and your own country's policies regarding studying outside of your country for a university degree.

Contact the American Embassy or Consulate in your country to get the forms required for U.S. study. This process will take more time than you expect, so go as early as possible. In most countries, first time student visa applicants are required to appear for an in-person interview. Make sure to bring all the appropriate documents with you at that time.

7. Consider the cost of studying in the United States.

In order to obtain a student visa, you will need to prove to the State Department that you are able to afford study in the United States. If you want to obtain both an undergraduate and a graduate degree, expect six to eight years of study.

You will need a minimum of US $12,000 per year; many universities cost more than $20,000 per year. You must plan for the total cost of living and studying for a number of years. Remember to add in a five percent (5%) annual increase in tuition and related fees when you are estimating costs. For example:

If you pay $23,000 for tuition, fees, books, housing, transportation, food and essentials in the 1999–2000 school year, the cost will be $24,150 in the 2001–2002 school year, and $25,375 in the 2002–2003 school year.

Financial scholarships and aid are rare for international students at the undergraduate level, and are very limited at the graduate level.

Most American students need additional support to finance their education. Many take loans, part-time work-study jobs, and teaching and research assistantships. What kinds of loans and/or work-study programs does your country offer as support? You might want to call the Department or Ministry of Education to ask about possible assistance for your education.

- If you are applying for undergraduate school, you may want to take the SAT to determine your skill level.
- If you are applying to graduate school, you may want to register to take the GRE or GMAT to get an idea of what your level is.
- At the end of this year, take another TOEFL exam to see how much progress you have made.

One Year Before Admission Target Date

This is a very critical year. During this year you should do the following:

September

1. Narrow down the list of the universities to which you seriously want to apply. We recommend choosing five schools: two schools you are sure you will be

admitted to, and three schools you hope to get into but are not certain about. Begin to collect the information and documents you'll need for the application.

2. Be sure to check the application deadlines dates for each of your five schools. Deadlines can vary widely: some may be as early as November, and others may be as late as February. Do not assume that all application deadline dates are the same.

3. Every school application requires different things of you, so make sure that you are clear about what you will need to send. The most common application items are:

   • A properly completed application, signed by you, the applicant

   • Two or three "letters of recommendation"
   A letter of recommendation is a personal reference by someone who personally recommends your abilities to excel.

   • Official academic records
   Academic records include official copies of school transcripts and diplomas. Arrange for English translation of your transcripts if a school requests this.

   • Report of your test scores

   • A personal statement (essay) written by you

   • An application fee (payable in U.S. dollars)

   • Evidence of financial resources necessary to complete your studies

4. Research and register for any exams you need to take.

October and November

1. Take the appropriate tests necessary.

2. If your TOEFL score is below 550 on the paper and pencil TOEFL, or 213 on the computer-based TOEFL, intensify your English studies.

3. Try to find some American exchange students studying at your local university so that you can practice your spoken English.

4. Read an American newspaper or magazine.

5. If you have not yet received all your application information, fax or email the admissions offices of the schools from which you need additional documents.

December

1. December is usually a slow month at American universities and colleges. At most schools, there is an extended vacation period and semester break from mid-December until early January, so it may be difficult to contact the admissions office during that time.

Personal Checklist

Complete the following checklist to keep track of the admissions process.

❑ Take TOEFL for initial assessment

❑ Get the TOEFL score needed

❑ Learn about entrance exams needed (such as SAT, GRE, GMAT)

❑ Research and select five schools to apply to

❑ Obtain applications, catalogs, and scholarship and fellowship information from selected schools

❑ Check on visa requirements for studying abroad

❑ Investigate sources of financial aid

❑ Make financial plans to cover expenses

❑ Check deadlines for each school you have selected

❑ Identify people who can give references (e.g., teachers, employers)

❑ Request letters of recommendation and official transcripts

❑ Register for the exams necessary

❑ Study for and take the exams

❑ Begin a draft of essay(s) for your applications

❑ Be sure your academic records, letters of recommendation, & standardized test scores have been sent

❑ Revise/edit your essays

❑ Mail your applications with all requested documents

❑ Decide which school you will attend and confirm your attendance with Admissions Office

❑ Go to the embassy or consulate for F-1 visa

❑ Visit the doctor for any necessary immunizations and copies of health record

❑ Obtain information on health and travel insurance

❑ Arrange for necessary funds to be transferred to the United States

2. Spend this time gathering all remaining documents that the university has requested.

3. Arrange to have your transcripts and financial documentation sent to the schools on your list.

4. Work on getting your functional and communicative English skills in the best possible shape.

5. Draft a personal statement (personal essay) for your university applications.

6. Check to be sure that your test scores have been sent to all the colleges on your list.

7. If the admission deadline date is during the month of November or December, complete and mail your application with all requested documents to the universities of your choice. Make yourself a copy of the entire application in case it gets lost in the mail.

January

1. Prepare your applications with all necessary documents.

February

1. Complete all of your applications, financial worksheets, and essays.

2. Send your completed applications (send them via registered mail, if possible, so that you can be sure they are delivered). It is important that you keep copies of all your applications in case they get lost in the mail.

3. Check that the institutions and/or individuals you have asked to send recommendation letters, transcripts, and standardized test scores have done so.

March

1. Respond immediately and completely to any requests for more information from the universities on your list.

2. Review and solidify your financial plan, and make a plan for achieving it.

April and May

1. You should receive notification from the universities you have applied to, whether they accept you or not.

2. Decide which school you would like to attend. Make sure that you reply to all universities regarding your decision. Do not assume that they will hold a place for you if you do not officially reply by the requested date.

3. You should receive your I-20 shortly after you send in your acceptance of the offer from the admissions office. You may have to pay a deposit to the university before an I-20 document is issued.

4. You will be able to enter the United States 60 days before the date indicated on your I-20, so begin to make appropriate arrangements. You may want to go to the United States early:

   - To find housing
   - To adjust to the culture
   - To get used to hearing and using English
   - To get familiar with the campus and the local area

5. Go to the U.S. Embassy or Consulate to apply for an F-1 student visa.

6. Make airlines reservations for your departure.

June

1. Decide what kind of clothing you will need for the entire year in the United States.

2. Obtain information on health and travel insurance.

3. Get all necessary immunization shots and have copies of your health records.

4. Prepare to send your belongings to the university.

5. Arrange to have necessary funds transferred to the United States. The university can supply you with information regarding banking and finances.

6. Obtain traveler's checks.

July

1. Relax and enjoy time with your family before leaving.

2. Continue to study your English.

August

1. Arrive on campus in time for new international student orientation. This is an important event that will help you to adjust and succeed in your degree program. Do not miss it.

Types of Schools in the United States

St. Olaf College

Types of Schools in the United States

2

Americans tend to use the words *school, college*, and *university* interchangeably when talking about institutions of higher education, though each word technically is defined as something distinct. For example, you may frequently hear conversations like these:

Donna: "What *school* do you go to?"
Brent: "I go to Harvard."
Julie: "Do you enjoy *college* life?"
Maude: "Yeah. The social life at Penn State is great!"
Richard: "Are you happy that you have completed your *university* education?"
Carol: "Yes, but I will really miss my *college* friends."

Here are a few guidelines for understanding how Americans use these terms in the titles of educational institutions:

School and **academy** describe primary and secondary educational institutions (also known as K–12 institutions). The word college never refers to a primary or secondary school. Examples are: Keio Academy of New York, Thomas Jefferson High School, Phillips Andover Academy.

School is also used in the titles of professional, degree-granting divisions of universities, such as the School of Law, School of Business, or School of Medicine. Examples: Harvard Business School, UCLA School of Medicine.

College describes a post-secondary institution that offers a bachelor's degree. It also describes a division within a university that offers courses in a specific area. We speak of liberal arts colleges, teacher's colleges, and colleges of general studies. Examples: Amherst College, Columbia College.

University describes an institution that is composed of several colleges and schools. Examples: Harvard University, which includes Harvard College (the undergraduate institution), as well as Harvard Business School, Harvard Medical School, Harvard Law School (graduate institutions).

Did you know the following facts about four-year undergraduate study in the United States?

1. The first two years of an undergraduate degree are usually spent taking general education courses: English composition, history, science, math, languages, and social sciences. The second two years focus more on courses in the major field of study.

2. Students are able to take elective courses outside their majors in order to obtain a well-rounded education.

3. Some students choose a *double major*, which means that they receive a degree in two major fields of study.

4. A student accumulates approximately 30 credits per academic year, leading to the 120 credits needed to earn an undergraduate degree.

5. Students must normally maintain a 2.0 grade point average (with 4.0 being the highest) in order to remain in good academic standing at school.

6. Extracurricular activities such as athletics, theater, and music are considered to be a major part of undergraduate study.

7. Unlike other systems of education around the world, American students do not take comprehensive exams in order to qualify for a degree. Instead, they accumulate credits and take frequent exams on the material they are currently studying.

8. There are very few scholarships available for international students to study in the United States at the undergraduate level.

UNDERGRADUATE EDUCATION

In the United States, students complete 12 years of education before beginning higher education. *Primary* education takes place in the elementary and middle years. *Secondary* education, called high school, begins around grade 7–9, and ends with graduation in the 12th grade, or year, of formal schooling. Most students complete secondary education at about the age of 18.

The first level of higher education is called *postsecondary* education. Most often, students pursue a four-year undergraduate degree, called a *bachelor's degree*, though some students choose to pursue two-year degrees at community colleges or vocational schools. The undergraduate experience is at the heart of the American higher education system. Almost half of all international students who come to this country enroll as undergraduates.

GRADUATE EDUCATION

There are over 1,000 accredited graduate degree programs in the United States. Almost half of all international students studying in this country are pursuing graduate degrees. Graduate education involves a high level of original research and scholarship. Students generally work closely with one or two professors who share the same research interests. This is why it is very important to select a school based on the faculty in your field of study rather than on a prestigious name.

Master's candidates usually have to write a lengthy thesis based on original work and/or take comprehensive exams in order to qualify for the degree. *Doctoral* (Ph.D.) candidates must write dissertations based on original research and must defend their dissertations orally before a faculty committee. Graduate school courses are frequently small group seminars where the student is expected to participate in class discussion with the professor.

There are many opportunities for international graduate students to qualify for grant money, financial aid, teaching, or research fellowships within American graduate degree programs. A word of advice, however: In order to qualify for teaching assistantships, you must have very good oral presentation skills in English.

THE TWO-YEAR COLLEGE SYSTEM IN THE UNITED STATES

The *community college* system in the United States has recently attracted a lot of attention from international students. Community colleges are two-year, public, postsecondary institutions that offer certificate, diploma, and associate degree programs geared toward occupations and professions and toward helping students prepare to transfer to bachelor's degree programs. These institutions serve both traditional age students and adults, and provide opportunities for people to earn high school equivalency certificates, take occasional courses for personal or professional benefit, or enroll in full programs of studies.

Community colleges are located in every community across America and are usually easier to gain admission to than four-year institutions. Some international students like to begin their studies at these schools and then transfer after two years to a four-year school. Community colleges, junior colleges, vocational schools, and technical schools also offer some interesting, career-related majors that you may not find at a four-year college or university.

Examples are: hotel and restaurant management, travel and tourism industry, and training programs for x-ray technicians or automotive mechanics.

Many community college systems have open-admission policies, which means that they will accept all students with high school diplomas regardless of test scores and grade point averages. It is a way of giving American students a second chance if they didn't work as hard as they should have in high school. There is usually no financial aid or scholarship money available for international students to study at a two-year community college. If you expect to transfer from a community college to a four-year school, you'll need excellent English skills and very good grades.

ACADEMIC DEGREES

U.S. institutions of higher education award a variety of degrees. Here are the most common:

Associate's Degree

A two-year degree begun after completing 12 years of primary and secondary school. It is offered through a public community college, private junior college, regular undergraduate college, or technical college. (Example: A.S., Associate of Science)

Bachelor's Degree

A four-year degree begun after completing 12 years of primary and secondary school. It is offered at a private, liberal arts college or a public or private university that also offers graduate and professional programs. (Example: B.S., Bachelor of Science)

Professional Degree

A two or three-year degree begun only after completing a four-year bachelor's degree. It is offered through a public or private university. (Examples: M.B.A., Master of Business Administration; M.D., Doctor of Medicine)

Master's Degree

A one to three-year degree involving original research begun only after completing the 4-year bachelor's degree. It can be obtained through private liberal arts colleges and universities that offer graduate and professional programs. (Example: M.A., Master of Arts)

Doctorate Degree

A three to six-year degree involving original research after the completion of the bachelor's or the master's degree. It can be obtained through a university that offers graduate and professional programs. (Examples: Ph.D., Doctor of Philosophy; Ed.D., Doctor of Education)

Postdoctoral Study and Research

"Postdoc" research is reserved for scholars already in possession of a Ph.D., and can be arranged at a university that offers graduate and professional programs.

Certificate Program

Though not an official degree, a certificate program is a sequence of specialized courses in one subject area. They are generally offered through virtually all types of schools. (Examples: interior design, book publishing)

American Education Systems:
Different Routes to the Same Goals

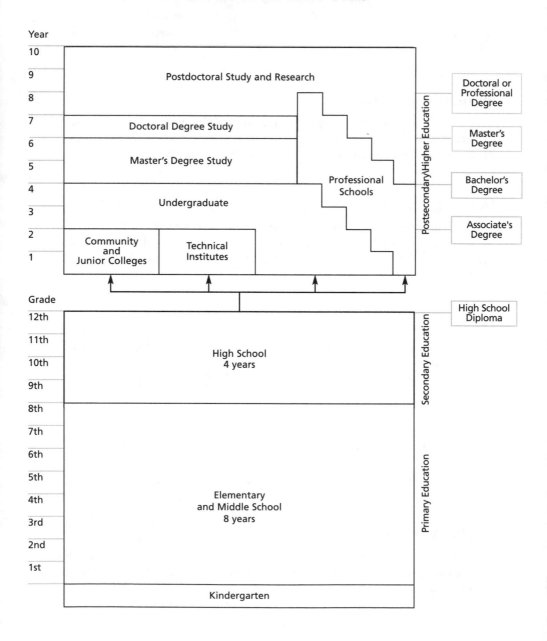

NONTRADITIONAL FORMS OF HIGHER EDUCATION AND DIPLOMA MILLS

There are many nontraditional programs of very high quality available in the United States. These programs include short-term training, certificate programs, correspondence courses, online or distance education courses, and credit for life experience programs (CLEP).

These programs are usually designed to accommodate busy working adults, those living in remote regions, or people unable to visit the campus due to an illness or disability. They are short-term, part-time, nondegree, and nonresidential, which is what makes them different than traditional degree programs on university campuses. Listed below are a few types of nontraditional programs:

Type of Program	Where It Is Offered	Length of Time
Residential nondegree programs	adult/university extension	one year or less
Professional certificate programs	university extension	12–18 months
Personal enrichment training	adult/university extension	several months
Short-term training/internships	various agencies	several months
Nonresidential and nondegree programs	internet and correspondence	varies
Residential degree/weekend/evening/summer	universities/colleges	unusual timing
External degree programs	internet and correspondence	varies

Diploma mills, on the other hand, are fraudulent institutions that take freedom of choice to an extreme. You may have seen an advertisement in your local newspaper that indicates you can earn an American bachelor's, master's, or Ph.D. degree with very little work or by having your "life experience" evaluated. Do not believe it! These are illegal organizations, and the U.S. government and the Federal Bureau of Investigation (FBI) are trying to put them out of business.

Many diploma mills target international students, so beware. As Americans are fond of saying, "There is no such thing as a free lunch." If the program sounds too easy, or as if you will get something for nothing without a lot of work, it is probably a sign that the program is not legitimate. Don't waste your money.

Always rely on the advice of an educational advisor to help you distinguish the reputable nontraditional programs from the diploma mills. Also, remember that it is better to go to accredited institutions than to those that are not accredited.

Fields of Study

University of California—Sant Cruz

Fields of Study **3**

Choosing a field of study, or what is called *your major*, is one of the most important decisions you will make in your preparation to study in this country. Your choice of major will affect your career path and future in many ways.

You may find that you are not certain about what major to choose. Although many people know early on what career paths they'll follow, many others are less certain. If you have a government scholarship to study accounting, for instance, the choice is simple. If not, your choices are more open.

You should know that many American students change their majors before graduation. This is a feature of the U.S. educational system that is not familiar to many international students. In this country, it is possible to change fields of study without having to start over at the beginning of your study, and it is frequently done. This is especially easy during the first year or two of undergraduate education. However, changing majors becomes more difficult as you progress. If you do find that you are unhappy with your choice of major, however, do not worry; the guidance counseling system at U.S. schools is very strong and supportive, so you will not be left without assistance.

Some people make the mistake of choosing a field of study and career that is not realistic. Be careful not to base your career choice on wishes and dreams unless you have a clear idea about how you will succeed. Factors to consider are: What kind of job will you be able to obtain with a certain degree? Is it a growing field or one that is in decreasing demand? How much time and financial resources do you have to commit?

As you evaluate your possible courses of study, consider how specific majors lead to various career opportunities. Here are just a few:

Major	Careers
Mathematics	Computer engineering; computer programming; software design; systems analysis; financial services; financial forecasting; financial analysis; banking; stockbroker
Biology	Doctor; physician's assistant; nurse; biologist; hospital or clinic technician
Chemistry	Chemical engineer; geneticist; pharmacist; geologist
Physics	Meteorologist; astronaut; astronomer; physicist
Foreign languages	Translator; linguist; teacher; foreign correspondent
Writing	Author; journalist; editor; publisher; teacher; speech writer; broadcaster; advertising executive
History	Historian; teacher
Visual arts	Graphic artist; illustrator
Botany	Forester; botanist; landscape architect
Political science	Lawyer; legislator; politician

THE STRUCTURE OF UNDERGRADUATE STUDY

The typical undergraduate program takes two years for an associate's degree, or four years for a bachelor's degree. A bachelor's degree is far more common than is an associate's degree.

Years One and Two

The *lower division* (generally the first two years) of a bachelor's degree includes three kinds of classes: Premajor requirements, general education requirements, and elective courses.

Premajor courses

Premajor courses are basic preparation for later, more specialized study. Almost every field of study has lower-division preparation requirements. For example, every business major includes basic courses in economics, accounting, math, and business law. These courses are usually taken during the first two years, before a student decides to concentrate in management, marketing, finance, accounting or one of the other concentrations available in business. All engineering students study mathematics, physics, and chemistry in the lower division before specializing in the third and fourth years.

General Education Requirement

During the first two years of undergraduate study, students are expected to take subjects that are *not related* to their major field of study. Almost every school has a requirement that students have exposure to academic areas quite different from the major field. This can be called *general education, distribution requirements* or *liberal arts requirements*. These requirements are the result of a liberal arts philosophy (short for "liberal arts and sciences") that is a unique feature of the United States: U.S. education believes that all undergraduate students should develop their verbal, written, and reasoning skills. The goal is to provide students with a broad understanding of the world.

The general education requirement is often misunderstood by international students who come from systems in which postsecondary work is intensively specialized from the beginning. Engineering students may not understand why they must take courses in music or history. Students in dramatic arts may be confused by the requirement to take a mathematics class. This emphasis on general education is a fundamental characteristic of undergraduate education in this country. While most of the general education courses are completed during the first two years, there may also be some upper-division requirements. However, there is no standard number of courses that are required by a particular college. Numbers may vary from as few as six courses to as many as 15.

At most schools, students have a great deal of flexibility in which general education courses must be taken. For example, in the area of arts and humanities, you may be able to choose from a group that contains three art courses, two music courses, one humanities class, and five modern language courses. The timing is also flexible; you (along with your adviser) may choose a pattern that is compatible with your schedule of major courses, which may be more fixed.

*A semester unit **is a measurement of the workload of a particular course, usually based on 1 unit per hour of lecture per week. Units are also called credits or hours.***

Transferring Credit

One area of confusion about general education has to do with *transferring credit*. Perhaps you have completed two years of school toward a polytechnic diploma in your home country. How much credit will you receive toward a degree in the United States? You may be told that two years of lower-division credit will be given, but that you must still complete the general education requirement. That will be in addition to the specialized upper-division study in your major field. General education may be as much as 60 percent of the courses you take in the first two years of undergraduate study, so you might have to spend an additional year to complete the general education requirement.

A typical general education pattern for the first two years might look like the following. A total of 36 semester units taken over two years from the list below:

Communication and Critical Thinking (9 units)

Choose one from each group:

Group 1: Public Speaking
Small Group Discussion

Group 2: Written Composition
Critical Writing

Group 3: Logic
Critical Thinking
Critical Thinking in the Social Sciences

The Physical Universe and Its Life Forms (9 units)

Choose one from each group:

Group 1: Astronomy
Chemistry
Geology
Oceanography
Physics

Group 2: Anatomy
Cultural Anthropology
Biology
Physiology

Group 3: Math for General Education
College Algebra
Calculus
Statistics

Arts, Literature, Philosophy, and Foreign Language (9 units)

Choose one from each group:

Group 1: Art, Dance, Drama, Music, Photography
Introduction to Drama
Music Appreciation
Introduction to Photography

Group 2: Basic News Writing
Literature
Humanities
Philosophy
Women's Studies

Group 3: Any lower-division Modern Language
Social, Political and Economic Institutions

Choose one from each group:

Group 1: Early U.S. History
Late U.S. History
Women in American History

Group 2: U.S. Government
Comparative Government

Group 3: Cultural Anthropology
Microeconomics
Macroeconomics
Cultural Geography
History of Europe
History of Western Civilization
History of Western Civilization 2
General Psychology
Human Sexuality
Social Psychology
Introduction to Sociology
Marriage and Family
Lifelong Understanding and Self-Development

Hot New Majors in the United States

E-Commerce: Internet businesses aren't just for M.B.A. graduates. Undergraduates are hungry to get involved, too, and colleges are creating e-commerce programs.

Cultural Studies: American society is changing, and with it, college curricula. Programs in Asian American and Latin American culture are booming, driven by new scholarship and demographics in the United States.

Neuroscience: Combining cellular and molecular biology with physics, chemistry, psychology and physiology, neuroscience is one of the new interdisciplinary degrees.

Cognitive Science: Related to neuroscience, this major is less about brain biology and more about reasoning, behavior, language, and logic.

Informatics: Informatics is the more "current" version of Information Technology by exploring social, ethical, and practical issues arising out of the technological revolution. One rapidly growing offshoot: bioinformatics, which combines computing with microbiology to analyze growing amounts of genomic and biological information.

Management Science and Engineering: As one professor in this field explained, "In civil engineering, students learn how to build a bridge. In our department, students learn whether to build a bridge."

Digital Arts and Multimedia Design: Someone's got to design all those new Web pages out there.

Adapted from "The Hot New Majors," by Yuval Rosenberg, Kaplan-Newsweek *How to Get Into College 2001*.

Choose classes that total at least 3 units:

> Environmental Biology (3 units)
> Child Development (4 units)
> First Aid (2 units)
> Humanities (3 units)
> Nutrition (3 units)
> Career Guidance (1 unit)

Elective courses

Electives are courses not required in general education or premajor programs. Students usually have free choice of such classes. Whether or not a student takes elective courses depends on the time she has available. In some fields, nearly 100 percent of a student's time is taken up by requirements. However, in other majors, most of the work is done only after entering the third year of undergraduate study. Typically, students have time for one or two elective classes each year.

Lower division-requirements typically include 60 units (or credit hours) of course work. Many universities require up to 70 units of lower division classes toward completion of the bachelor's degree, so there is some flexibility.

If a student is interested in doing so, he may be able to complete the first two years of a bachelor's degree at one school and then move (or transfer) to another school for the final two years. Transfer students can normally complete their degrees in the same number of years as students who stay at one school. This is common among students who begin at a two-year community college, then transfer to four-year schools to complete their bachelor's degrees.

Years Three and Four

In the third and fourth years of bachelor's degree study—also called the ***upper division***—students spend up to 90 percent of their time on specialized courses within the major field. Classes are often small, and students work closely with individual professors. These are the basic professional foundation classes in a major field.

Core Major Courses

After the common premajor courses are taken during the first two years, programs are broken down into more specialized fields. For example, most business majors will have taken prebusiness classes in years one and two, including calculus, two courses in accounting, one in business law, one in statistics, one or two in computer science and two in economics. For years three and four, these students will study more specialized areas of business, such as management, marketing, accounting, and finance. Each specialization will have intensive course work.

THE STRUCTURE OF GRADUATE STUDY

Graduate study (or *postgraduate study*, as it is sometimes called, generally follows the bachelor's degree for those who are pursuing advanced academic work. It includes the master's degree, such as the Master of Arts or the Master of Business Administration (M.B.A.), and the doctorate degree, often the Doctor of Philosophy (Ph.D.) in many fields, or the specialized doctorates such as the Doctor of Medicine (M.D.).

Study at the graduate level is highly specialized, and admission is usually very selective. Some graduate degrees require work experience before beginning the degree, and others do not. Unlike undergraduate education, there is no general education requirement in graduate study. This may be an advantage to you if you have completed undergraduate studies in your home country and you are entering the U.S. system at the graduate level. You might find, however, that there are certain undergraduate prerequisites you have not met for graduate study, and as a result, that you have to take some undergraduate classes before beginning graduate work.

Course work at the graduate level is demanding. A typical undergraduate program includes 15 or 16 units each semester, and the typical graduate program includes 9–12 units. Unlike most undergraduate classes, graduate work is primarily done with the guidance and supervision of a single professor. In addition, graduate students are often required to participate in group projects and seminars, requiring excellent communication skills and the ability to work as part of a scholarly team.

A master's degree usually requires two to three years of full-time study after completing a bachelor's degree. In addition to course work, students must write a long research paper (a *thesis*), demonstrating an ability to comprehend and apply professional research in the chosen field of study. Some programs also require an oral examination.

A doctorate (usually a Ph.D.) may take up to seven years. Some doctoral programs include a master's degree program, which students begin directly after the bachelor's

---

Did you know the following facts about studying in the United States?

- It is easy and common for students to change their majors during their undergraduate education.

- The certified public accountant (CPA) system used in the United States is quite different from the system used in other countries.

- In a typical year, fewer than 1% of international applicants are accepted into U.S. medical schools.

- Employment prospects for dentistry are decreasing in the United States, but may be increasing in other countries.

---

degree. The candidate then continues through course work and intermediate qualifying examinations. Other doctoral programs require the completion of a master's degree before beginning doctoral studies.

Course work and intermediate exams are required in all doctoral study programs. In addition, a doctoral candidate must prepare a **dissertation** (a final research project) under the supervision of a faculty advisor. This dissertation is a major step in the completion of the doctoral degree, and the candidate is expected to produce an original and significant contribution to his field of study.

Once the course work for a doctoral program has been finished, many candidates complete their research in a job outside the university campus. A doctoral candidate who has completed all the required course work and intermediate exams is sometimes referred to as **ABD**, or "all but dissertation."

Unlike the doctoral process in some countries, dissertation work in the United States is not done as part of a research project designed by a supervising professor. Rather, the doctoral candidate alone is responsible for defining and implementing the research, though the professor provides critical guidance. The candidate must also revise the research as needed to meet the dissertation approval requirements. As a final step, a doctoral candidate must orally defend, or argue for, her research in front of a faculty committee.

FIELDS OF STUDY

Listed below are some popular fields of study for international students in the United States.

Popular Majors for International Students

- *Accounting*
- *Agriculture*
- *Applied Mathematics*
- *Business Management*
- *Computer Science*
- *Economics*
- *Engineering*
- *Health Sciences*
- *International Studies*
- *Law*
- *Medicine*

Agriculture

The career area of agriculture includes agricultural science; animal husbandry and genetic engineering; food science and nutrition; botany and plant sciences; agricultural engineering; and agricultural technology.

Agricultural science is related to biological science. Agricultural scientists study farm animals and crops, soil and water conservation, bringing food to consumer markets, pest control, and ways to improve agricultural yields. Agricultural scientists may perform basic and applied research in university or corporate laboratories, or they may work for government agencies. They often work as *consultants* (contract specialists) helping agricultural producers.

Animal husbandry specialists generally specialize in the development of better means of producing and processing meat, poultry, and dairy products.

Food scientists develop better ways of processing, storing, and delivering food. They may also work in product development or basic agricultural production research. Nutritionists may work for governments helping to protect food supplies by enforcing sanitation and quality regulations.

Plant scientists study the management and improvement of crops, including new ideas in genetic engineering.

Soil scientists study the biological and physical composition of soil and often advise farmers on fertilizers and crop rotation. They may work with construction engineers to provide technical support, and with environmental scientists.

Agricultural fields require various levels of training. A bachelor's degree may qualify an agricultural scientist for some lower-level positions. Generally, a master's degree or higher is necessary for research. A Ph.D. is usually needed for teaching and administrative positions, although this varies from country to country. Those with backgrounds in the newest phases of agriculture, such as genetic engineering, biotechnology, and molecular biology, will have employment advantages.

Since so much of the work of agricultural scientists is done in consultation with others, communication skills and the ability to work with others are important factors in success.

Employment in the area of agricultural science is expected to grow fairly rapidly in less developed countries of the world, and will probably maintain a steady pace in better-developed agricultural economies. Employment venues are mainly in government and university offices. However, some private corporations that specialize in food and beverage production may have opportunities as well. Earning potential will vary with education, but for most people it will reflect the average government and university pay in each country. Higher earnings are often available in the private sector.

Agricultural technology is the area of professional support services for the agricultural sciences discussed above. Agricultural technicians provide laboratory support in food, plant and animal research, and in conducting tests to improve crop or animal yields and disease resistance. Positions for agricultural technicians usually require a minimum of a two-year associate's degree. Many agricultural technicians continue on to the bachelor's degree (four-year degree) level.

A typical course schedule for an agriculture science major might include:
> General Chemistry (5 units)
> Plant Genetics (4 units)
> Experimental Design and Analysis (4 units)
> Chemistry Calculations (1 unit)
> World Food Production Systems (4 units)
> Multivariate Systems and Modeling (4 units)
> Domestic Animals (4 units)
> Microbiology (4 units)
> Plant Population Biology (3 units)
> Microbiology Laboratory (3 units)

Applied Mathematics

The field of mathematics has become increasingly popular with international students. One reason for this popularity may be that many people consider secondary-level math instruction in the United States to be less advanced than in many other countries. Whether or not this is true is debatable. Nevertheless, the opportunities for trained mathematicians are very real. The fields of applied mathematics and pure mathematics are growing worldwide with the exponential advancement of technology.

The career area of mathematics includes: actuary science; statistics; business management; accounting; and economics.

An *actuary* or *actuarial scientist* works with mathematical situations involving the future. These problems include insurance risk (life expectancy, credit and debt, health potentials) and investment strategies (public and private investments, capital outlooks, economic strategies analysis). Usually, actuaries specialize in one professional area: insurance, financial planning and investing, or pensions. An actuary is expected to have at least a bachelor's degree, although many actuaries have advanced degrees in either pure or applied mathematics. The field of actuarial science has special features to consider.

1. There are professional societies that administer qualification examinations in areas of actuarial science: probability, calculus, linear algebra, risk theory actuarial mathematics, and statistics.
2. Some exams must be passed before completing your bachelor's degree in order to obtain a favorable position in the job market.
3. Some specialized examinations in actuarial science can take up to ten years to complete (most actuaries complete them in seven or eight years). You must usually complete your specialization series in order to advance to the fellowship level of your society.
4. The good news is that, because of these professional societies and their influence on job qualification standards, advanced degrees in mathematics are somewhat less important in this field than in other fields of applied mathematics, such as accounting or statistics.

Starting salaries for actuaries are slightly above average. Salaries for experienced actuaries (especially those who have completed their professional exams) are much higher than average.

A typical major course schedule for actuarial study might include:

Calculus I (4 units)
Mathematical Statistics (3 units)
Mathematics of Insurance (3 units)
Mathematics of Life Contingencies (3 units)
Numerical Analysis (3 units)
Mathematical Probability (3 units)
Advanced Theory of Interest (3 units)

A *statistician* is an applied mathematician who concentrates on the collection and analysis of data. Much of the work of a statistician is done with computers, developing information about trends, probabilities, and projections of future activities. Statisticians work with business managers, economists, sociologists, and other social scientists. Together, they develop statistical research that can be used in experimental studies being performed by others.

While entry-level jobs are available once you complete your bachelor's degree in mathematics or statistics, higher-level employment usually requires a master's degree or a Ph.D. Some employers may prefer those with graduate or professional degrees in fields related to statistics. For example, an applicant with a bachelor's degree in statistics and a Master of Business Administration may be more desirable to an employer than an applicant with both a bachelor's and a master's degree in statistics alone.

Earnings for statisticians, especially those with advanced degrees, are well above average in the private sector.

A typical major course schedule for statistics might include:

Calculus (4 units)
Mathematical Studies (4 units)
Regression Analysis (3 units)
Fortran for Applied Mathematics (3 units)
Mathematical Probability (3 units)
Advanced Probability (3 units)
Numerical Analysis (4 units)
Analysis of Variance (3 units)
Statistical Data Analysis (3 units)

Business, Management, and Accounting

The academic areas of business are complex. What most people mean by "business" is often not well defined, as business can be applied to many things. A "business" major at an American university can include any of the following specialties, among others: management; accounting; marketing; finance; and information systems.

Management is an area with many specializations, such as hotel management, construction management, or health services management. This chapter will deal with general management, but you should be aware that each specialized area of management has its own academic and training requirements and opportunities.

Managers are professionals who plan and carry out policies in business and service organizations. A manager may select, train, and supervise personnel, and as he gains responsibility, will perform more supervisory functions. If one is managing a small business, he may have wider responsibilities. He may manage the staff; be responsible for accounting costs, profits and losses; and perform many of the daily operations of the company.

Travel is often associated with corporate management. Managers may also be transferred to field offices in different regions in which the company does business.

At the professional level, the majority of managers have a bachelor's degree, and quite often a master's degrees (often an M.B.A.). This requirement varies widely, however, and there are many managers, especially in smaller business, who do not have university degrees. In many cases, managers hold degrees in areas other than business, such as public administration or economics, while some have bachelor's degrees in other fields, such as engineering or computer information systems, and have continued their education for M.B.A. degrees.

Job prospects for managers depend on the economy of the country in which they are seeking employment. In general, there are more entry-level positions available than advanced positions, and there are more positions in locations where new businesses are opening or where multinational companies are expanding.

Earnings for entry-level and middle managers are average. As managers are promoted within larger companies, salaries improve greatly, with top managers among the highest paid workers in the world.

A typical major course schedule for management might include:

Business Finance (3 units)
Management Accounting (3 units)
Financial Accounting (3 units)
Data Analysis for Managers (3 units)
International Operations Management (3 units)
Microeconomics (3 units)
Principles of Marketing (3 units)
Issues in Productivity Management (3 units)
Calculus for Business (3 units)
Operations Management (3 units)
General Psychology (3 units)
Presentational Speaking (3 units)

Accountants work with financial reports, spreadsheets, and databases; verify financial data; prepare tax documents; and keep track of business information systems. Some accountants work for government organizations, auditing businesses who must comply with government regulations. They may also maintain the records of government agencies. Other accountants work for corporations, where they analyze budgets and financial records. And other accountants choose to work in the public arena, assisting in the preparation of tax returns or consulting with companies. Internal auditors specialize in evaluating the management information systems within companies.

As an international student, you should be aware that the certified public accountant (C.P.A.) system used in this country is different from the accountancy systems used in many other countries. For example, in British-pattern economies, the chartered accountancy system is not directly compatible with the C.P.A. system. So someone who is trained in the American system may have to study for an additional year to practice in the United Kingdom.

The field of accounting has changed dramatically since computers were introduced. The days of pencil-and-paper accounting are obsolete, and a modern accountant must have a solid background in computing applications. Most employers require a minimum of a bachelor's degree, but preference is usually given to those with advanced training (either a C.P.A., a master's degree in accounting, or an M.B.A. with a concentration in accounting). More than in most fields, experience is very important in gaining employment in accounting, so if this is your field of study, consider doing an internship to get work experience while you are in school.

Earnings for entry-level accountants are average, although earnings for experienced accountants are above average. Employment prospects vary from country to country. In some places, there are more positions available in the public sector, and in other places, particularly in regions where private business is expanding, the private sector offers the best opportunities.

A typical major course schedule for accounting might include:

Calculus I (4 units)
Federal Tax Procedures (3 units)
Cost Analysis and Control (3 units)
Financial Accounting (3 units)
Intermediate Accounting (4 units)
Management Control Systems (3 units)
Macroeconomics (3 units)
Cost Accounting (3 units)
Special Problems in Accountancy (3 units)
Auditing (3 units)
Geology (4 units)
Business Law for Accountants (3 units)
Advanced Theory of Interest (3 units)

Computer Science, Database Administration, and Systems Analysis

Computer science and *computer engineering* are confusing terms. Each university defines the terms differently. For example, the people who design and build computers are usually called "computer engineers," but this field of study may be under the School of Engineering at one university and under the department of computer science at another. We will consider computer engineering as a branch of engineering in this chapter.

Computer scientists in academic settings generally work on the development of theoretical areas of computer operations, such as operating system language design and computational theory. Computer scientists in the private sector work with complex data management systems and with specialized applications, such as advanced graphics systems or advanced financial forecasting programs.

While there is no standard for preparation in computer science, it is usually expected that an academic position in the field requires at least a master's degree and more commonly a doctorate. A strong mathematics background is essential. There are more positions for holders of a bachelor's degree in the private sector, but even there, graduate degrees are often preferred. Experience can be very important in gaining employment, and employers often seek those with proven skills. An international student, especially at the graduate level, should consider applying for a research assistant position or participating in an internship while studying.

Earnings in computer science are average in academic positions, but higher in the private sector. Earnings tend to be higher for applicants with advanced degrees.

A typical major course schedule for computer science might include:

Digital Logic Design (3 units)
Advanced Database Management (3 units)
Intermediate Programming (4 units)
Computer Methods II (3 units)
Theory of Programming Languages (3 units)
Database Structures (3 units)
File Processing (4 units)
Advanced Compiler Design (3 units)
Calculus II (4 units)
Operating Systems (3 units)
Assembly Language Programming (3 units)

Database administration involves working with database systems, usually in the private sector. Database administrators develop systems to store and manipulate data. They are responsible for the efficiency and usefulness of the business information systems of companies, as well as for the security of data.

Database administrators may enter the field with a two-year associate's degree, but most employers prefer a bachelor's degree in computer science with special training in database management. Once again, experience is very important in finding a good job.

Earnings for entry-level database managers are average, and above average for experienced database administrators.

A typical major course schedule for an associate's degree in computer science might include:

Business Data Processing (3 units)
Systems Analysis and Design (3 units)
Statistics (3 units)
Financial Accounting (3 units)
Discrete Mathematics (3 units)

47

Systems analysis is the problem-solving area of computer science. Systems analysts plan the solutions to programming problems by working with managers and users to define needs and by working through the overall computer design (both hardware and software). Once the planning has been done, systems analysts explain the process to the users in understandable terms, develop the program, and test the actual system and its applications in a real-life setting.

Systems analysts are generally expected to have a bachelor's degree. If an analyst intends to work in a scientific field, a background in engineering, physical sciences or applied mathematics is preferred. For business fields, an academic background in management or management information systems might be required.

Worldwide growth in the area of systems analysis is expected to continue for many years. Earnings are above average at all levels and with all academic degrees.

Economics

Economists are social scientists interested in the economic activity of organizations, cities, and countries. They study the distribution of products and money, the activities of consumers, and patterns of domestic and international trade. Economists are often asked to predict future economic activity for government or business planning purposes. They design studies to predict this activity, and a lot of their work is in data collection and analysis. Economists make frequent use of computer models in their analysis and prediction of future activity.

Although it is possible to gain entry into the field with a bachelor's degree, economists at this level largely work in data collection. For more senior positions, an advanced degree is usually necessary. Many experienced economists work in independent consulting firms, and positions in such firms normally expect a Ph.D.

The professional field of economics is expanding, especially in computer modeling, and is expected to continue to grow in the future. Entry-level earnings with a bachelor's degree are below average for college-trained professionals, but earnings rise rapidly with experience and higher degrees.

A typical major course schedule for economics might include:

Statistics (3 units)
International Economic Relations (3 units)
Applied Economic Theory (3 units)
Microeconomics and Analysis (3 units)

Intermediate Macroeconomic Theory (3 units)
Monetary and Fiscal Policy (3 units)
Business Calculus (4 units)
History of Economic Thought (3 units)
Government Finance (3 units)
Comparative Economic Systems (3 units)
American Government (3 units)
Economic Research Methods (3 units)

Engineering

An *engineer* is someone who uses scientific knowledge to design solutions to practical problems.

Some engineers design machinery and commercial products; some build highways and bridges; some develop industrial processes; and some plan and supervise the construction of buildings. Other engineers analyze needs, create mechanical devices or operational systems to meet those needs, design and test their ideas or products, and supervise the production and maintenance of those products.

Clearly, this field is very complex. There are many occupations under the definition of engineer. At many universities, the school of engineering may offer degrees in aeronautical engineering, civil engineering, construction engineering, chemical engineering, electrical and computer engineering, industrial engineering, and mechanical engineering. In other words, to say, "I want to become an engineer" is not sufficient. Students must specialize in an area of engineering.

Fortunately, there are many common courses during the first two years of engineering study, and it is fairly easy to shift from one concentration to another. Any area of engineering will require math, chemistry, and physics. All engineers are expected to be familiar with the use of computers in solving problems. Engineers trained in one specialization may actually work in another. Flexibility is an important personal trait in this field.

In general, entry-level engineers are expected to hold a bachelor's degree in engineering from an accredited university. Many engineers go on for advanced degrees in order to increase their employment opportunities. Other engineers obtain advanced degrees in other fields, such as business management or law. It is common to find top business executives and government leaders who have undergraduate degrees in engineering.

Earnings for engineers are average at the entry level, but rise to above average with higher degrees and more experience. Engineers who have gone into management earn salaries that are much higher than average.

There are many more specializations in engineering than can be discussed here. However, some of the most common areas include:

Aerospace Engineering is the design and development of aircraft, military missiles, and spacecraft.

Chemical Engineering is the design and development of processes in the production of chemicals and pharmaceuticals.

Civil Engineering is the design and supervision of the construction of roads, buildings, bridges, dams and water resources.

Computer Engineering is the design and development of computer hardware, associate peripheral equipment, and network systems.

Electrical/Electronic Engineering is the design, development, and testing of electrical equipment, including power generation and transmission equipment, electric motors, lighting systems, and robotic controls.

Industrial Engineering is the planning of efficient means of manufacturing and production, including personnel management, business and organizational development, and technology utilization. Industrial engineers are less directly involved with products and processes than engineers in other areas.

Mechanical Engineering is the design and development of machines, tools, engines, refrigeration equipment, and other mechanisms that may be used by engineers. This is the broadest engineering specialty.

Nuclear Engineering is the design, development, and operation of applications within the field of nuclear energy in both military and public utility areas.

Petroleum Engineering is the exploration and development of oil or natural gas reserves, including optimized recovery systems.

A typical undergraduate major course schedule for aerospace, chemical, and civil engineering might include:

Space Systems Engineering (3 units)
Fluid Dynamics (3 units)
Dynamics (3 units)
Aerospace Structures (3 units)
Industrial Chemical Calculations (3 units)
Ordinary Differential Equations (3 units)
Mechanics of Materials (3 units)
Dynamics (3 units)
Hazardous Materials (3 units)
Construction Materials Lab (3 units)
Thermodynamics (3 units)
Engineering Communications (3 units)
Civil Engineering: Economic Analysis (3 units)
Transportation Engineering (3 units)
Engineering Graphics (3 units)

Health Sciences and Medicine

The study of *medicine* in the United States (leading to an M.D. degree) is based on an undergraduate preparatory degree and is taught only at the graduate level. This is different from most other countries, where the study of medicine begins at the undergraduate level. The differences can be substantial, and you should definitely consider this in your decision to study in the United States.

It is extremely difficult for an international student to be admitted into a U.S. medical school. In a typical year, fewer than one percent (1%) of qualified international applicants are admitted. While it is relatively easy for international students to enter premedical programs in preparation of studying medicine, it is far more difficult to be admitted into medical school.

There are several alternatives to consider when thinking about a medical career.

1. If you are not admitted to a medical school, will you be content to study in a related area such as microbiology, genetics, virology, anatomy, physiology, nursing, or medical laboratory technology?

2. If you are not admitted to a medical school, would you consider the alternative of an offshore medical school (usually set up to accommodate American students who cannot get into medical schools because of overcrowding)? Some students find this an acceptable path, while others regard it as risky.

3. Would you consider medical study in your own country with the possibility of advanced training in the United States after completing your M.D.? This may be an option if you expect to study specialized medicine. It may be easier to enter such programs in the United States.

Physicians diagnose and treat illness and injury. They prescribe medical treatment and order and evaluate medical diagnostic tests. They may work with patients in private offices, in hospitals, in clinics, or in research facilities.

If you would like to pursue a medical degree, make sure you study advanced mathematics, life sciences, and physical sciences in secondary school. Ordinarily, premedical study at the undergraduate level is similar to undergraduate study programs in chemistry or biology.

Preparation for the medical practice usually takes at least 11 years after completing secondary school:

- Four years of undergraduate preparation in a premedical program at a university
- Four years of medical school
- Three to eight years of supervised hospital residency in a medical specialization

In general, the tuition costs for medical study are very high, and earnings during internship and residency are low.

Employment prospects in medicine are very good, and the number of entrants to medical schools is declining but still very competitive. Some university counselors attribute this to the lower expectations of financial reward for doctors since the advent of managed health care in the United States.

Currently, the average U.S. physician earns around $150,000, making this one of the highest-paid occupations in the country. But in a changing world of managed health and health maintenance organizations (HMOs), this figure is expected to decline. Physicians in the United States work long hours. The average work week for a practicing doctor is about 60 hours.

A typical graduate major course schedule for medicine might include:

Cellular Biology (5 units)
Genetics (3 units)
Human Biology (8 units)
General Chemistry I (5 units)
Molecular Biology (3 units)
Introduction to Clinical Medicine (4 units)
English Composition (3 units)
Histological Techniques (2 units)
Introduction to Family Practice (3 units)
Calculus I (4 units)
Technical Writing in Biology (3 units)
Biological Illustration (3 units)

The field of *dentistry* is more open to international students than medicine, though it is still quite competitive and expensive. Dentistry is usually a four-year postgraduate field of study based on a predentistry major in an undergraduate institution. Some dental schools will consider applicants with two years of undergraduate predental study. Dentistry involves the prevention, diagnosis, and treatment of problems in teeth and gums, including specialized surgery as well as removal of decay, preventative treatment of healthy teeth, filling of cavities, and treatment of diseased teeth.

Employment prospects in dentistry are somewhat below average in the United States, though this may not be true in other countries with developing health care systems. Most dentists in the United States are self-employed, and earnings are well above average.

A typical graduate major course schedule for dental study might include:

Physics (4 units)
Organic Chemistry (5 units)
Head and Neck Anatomy (3 units)
Cellular Biology (5 units)
Microbiology (5 units)
Contemporary Dentistry (4 units)
General Chemistry (5 units)
Comparative Vertebrate Anatomy (5 units)
Biochemistry (2 units)
Medical Microbiology (2 units)
Communication in Dental Practice (1 unit)

The field of *registered nursing* in the United States has changed dramatically in recent years. Nurses function less as assistants who rely on doctors for direction and more as health care providers with a range of independent decisionmaking roles. While this is not true in all cases, it is likely to be an increasing characteristic of nurse training and practice in coming years. This is in some ways in contrast to the expectations of nurses in many countries and should be taken into account by international students considering nursing training in the United States.

Registered Nurses (called *R.N.s*) have a wide range of responsibilities and work situations. Most R.N.'s work in hospitals; others work in private offices, schools, and clinics, or as home health care or residential care nurses.

Nurses in the United States can continue their education to obtain a *nurse practitioner's* credential, which allows them to perform many of the same functions as practicing physicians and even to issue prescriptions in some states. The nurse practitioner and the physician's assistant (a very similar position) are relatively new medical professions in this country, but they offer an alternative for those who do not qualify for medical school.

Training for a career as an R.N. can take different educational tracks. Many R.N.s graduate from two-year programs, often at community colleges. Many others complete a B.S.N. (Bachelor's of Science in Nursing) at four-year colleges. A few nurses are trained in two to three-year "diploma" programs in hospitals. Each track leads to the same entry level, although B.S.N. nurses usually have advantages in terms of promotion and increased responsibilities. For this reason, many two-year nurses continue on to obtain a B.S.N. degree, even while working as an R.N. Those interested in administration and management may wish to go on to a master's degree (M.S.N.).

No matter which kind of degree is chosen, a nurse cannot work in any field without passing a rigorous licensing examination after completing formal study and supervised clinical experience.

The outlook for employment in the nursing field is generally strong worldwide. Increasingly technological applications within the profession may require new kinds of training, and the trend toward independent decision making by nurses is expected to grow. Pay is average for beginning professionals, with above-average pay for experienced nurses who take supervisory responsibility.

A typical lower-division undergraduate major course schedule for nursing might include:

Basic Skills of Nursing Practice (6 units)
Anatomy (4 units)
Nursing as a Career (1 unit)
Chemistry for Health Sciences I (5 units)
Nursing Laboratory Practicum (2 units)
Microbiology (4 units)
Lifetime Health Promotion (3 units)
General Psychology (3 units)

International Studies

International studies is a broad category that can lead to various careers, such as diplomacy, law, economics, or international student advising. While there are specialized programs in international studies, called *area studies*, and programs which focus on specific countries or regions, such as Latin America or Asia, there are no major occupations that are based solely on this field of study. It is not unusual to find a person with a bachelor's degree in international studies who has gone on for further degree study in another field. It is also common for holders of bachelor's degrees in other fields to work on master's degrees in international studies or one of its specializations.

A typical major course schedule in international studies might include:

English Composition (3 units)
International Trade (3 units)
Latin American Village Agriculture (1 unit)
United States History (3 units)
Global Politics (3 units)
Seminar in Latin American Studies (4 units)
Sociology (3 units)
Diversity and Change (3 units)
Methodology of Area Studies (4 units)
Basic Chemistry (4 units)
History of Modern Africa (3 units)
College Algebra (4 units)
Ethics (3 units)

A Few Words of Caution about Law

- The study of law in the United States is specific to the American legal system unless you are enrolled in an international law program. Check the curriculum carefully to be certain that you are enrolling in the program you want.

- In most countries, law is an undergraduate major. Undergraduate preparation in another country is not always appropriate preparation for entry into an American law school.

- Be realistic about the employment status of lawyers in your country who have been trained in the United States. Are they welcome in the public sector? Are they allowed to represent clients in civil or criminal cases?

Law

Like medicine, *law* is taught as a graduate program in this country. There are many prelaw programs at the undergraduate level, but admission to law school is not based on undergraduate majors. Rather, admission to law school is based on undergraduate grades, the strength of an undergraduate program, a personal interview, and, especially, the Law School Admission Test (LSAT) score. Law schools use their own formulas for admissions, and may have additional requirements. In general, students have completed a bachelor's degree prior to entry, and may even be expected to have some work experience.

A typical law school education after undergraduate studies is three years. Though most law students intend to practice as *attorneys* (also called *lawyers*), many people study law for other career reasons. For instance, a doctor might wish to understand the legal implications of his work, or an accountant might need special knowledge of tax law. Many legislators also have law degrees.

A practicing attorney might work in one of many legal areas such as: general civil law, tax and estate law, criminal law, corporate law, and family law.

Before a law school graduate can practice law in the United States, she must pass the *Bar Examination*. The Bar is a very rigorous exam: Only about half of the test takers pass it on the first try. The test can be repeated, and perhaps half of those who fail the first time pass on second or third attempts. In other words, completing law school is no guarantee of passing the Bar.

Lawyers may work in any of the areas discussed above. They are often *advisers* and *consultants*, assisting their clients in business and personal matters. They may act as *advocates*, presenting evidence and arguing for their clients in court. Lawyers are required to do intensive research and to document their work, so they must possess excellent research and communication skills. Lawyers are increasingly turning to computers for research and communications, so computer proficiency is becoming a necessity for those considering law as a profession.

Lawyers in the United States work very long hours. Earnings are average for entry-level professionals but can increase dramatically with experience and promotion within a law firm.

A typical major course schedule for law school might include:
Civil Procedure (3 units)
Contracts (3 units)
Criminal Law (3 units)
Legal Research and Writing (1 unit)
Legal Traditions (1 unit)
Torts I (3 units)

Selecting the Right School

University of Southern California

Selecting the Right School 4

Selecting the best school for you is, of course, an important process. The decision you make may affect the entire course of your life and career, and the choice should not be made in a hurry. There should be an orderly selection process that will give you the best chance of finding the right school for you to study and experience life in another culture. That's what this chapter will help you begin.

As we have mentioned, the U.S. Department of Education is not the single central authority for educational standards. Therefore, application deadlines vary from school to school. Similarly, response and notification times are not all the same, so while the steps discussed are generally true, exceptions do exist.

Allow sufficient time for the:
- **Exams you will need to take**
- **Recommendation letters you will need to assemble**
- **Kinds of investigation you will need to do**

GATHERING INFORMATION

Institutional Rankings

There is no official ranking of schools in the United States. There are several publications, however, that rank schools, comparing their quality and programs. While these listings can contain useful information, do not choose your school based on these rankings alone. Even the most informative rankings are not official, and it is difficult to know what criteria they use. In fact, many rankings are based on criteria that do not apply to international students. Famous rankings are compiled annually by *U.S. News & World Report*, *Money Magazine*, and *The Gourman Report*.

If the reputation of an institution is very important to you, make school rankings a part of your selection process. But remember that since there are more than 3,300 accredited colleges and universities, the "top 25" schools represent fewer than 1% of your choices!

Advisory Services

Advisory services, often connected with English language programs, can be of great assistance in helping you locate the best school. These types of services can be an essential resource.

Academic Resources

Does your local secondary school or university have someone who is familiar with the U.S. admissions process? There may also be an American university adviser at an English language school in your city. Another possibility is a U.S. Commission for International Educational Exchange, which many international cities have. Go to the website http://exchanges.state.gov/education/list.htm for a complete country listing.

Family and Friends

Ask around your circle of friends and family members to see if anyone has studied in the United States. And don't hesitate to ask any American friends you have to help you apply to U.S. schools.

Books and Electronic Resources

1. Is there a local book shop that carries English language books (perhaps the one where you bought this book)? It may carry a standard reference guide to university programs in the United States. (Does it have Kaplan's *College Catalog*?)

2. Is there a library in your city with reference materials on U.S. education? Perhaps a public library, or a private library at your school or university.

3. Do you have computer access to the internet? Most schools in the United States now have websites where you can get more information.

GETTING READY FOR THE SEARCH

As you begin your search for schools, there are a number of things to examine.

Field of Study

There are hundreds of fields of study available in the United States. Check to see if your major is available at the schools that interest you. If you are using a standard American college catalog, there is usually a section that lists majors and gives the names of the schools that offer that major. Or read the school's catalog (sometimes called a *prospectus*). Almost all universities have websites where you can do research. You can also see each American school's most popular fields of study in Kaplan's *College Catalog*.

As you do your research, look carefully at the names of majors. Sometimes two very different fields have similar names. For example, *engineering* and *engineering technology* are not the same, yet *biology* and *biological science* may be very similar.

As we have mentioned already, if you are not sure about your field of study, you might be able to enroll without an "undeclared major." And if you begin in a field that you are not happy with, it is possible to change majors, especially in the early undergraduate years. This is unlike the systems in many other countries, in which a student cannot change majors without starting all over again (if at all). Many American students change majors at least once before graduation.

Level of Study

Even if a major is offered by a college or university, you should confirm that the program is available at your level. It might be that a university (for example, Stanford) offers an M.B.A. but not a bachelor's degree. Another school may have an undergraduate program in chemistry but not a graduate-level program.

Admissibility of International Students

It is important to find out if a program has any restrictions on the admission of international students. For example, some state (public) universities have popular programs that are overcrowded (or *impacted*). A program such as physical therapy might be so crowded with qualified applicants that it is open only to permanent residents of that state. International students and residents of other states are not eligible, or their numbers may be limited. If you are not certain of the status of your major, ask the admissions office of the schools to which you are applying.

Academic Preparation

Most universities expect to see good grades in certain subjects before accepting you into an undergraduate major. If you are an engineering applicant, for instance, you should have a strong background in chemistry, physics, and mathematics. If your performance has been poor or if you have had minimal exposure to those subjects, you will not likely be accepted to study engineering or science, even if you have excellent grades in history, art, and economics.

How strong is the program in your major at the schools you have chosen? College rank may not be the only clue. Find out what courses are offered in your major and what credentials the professors have.

A very important part of your application will be your *transcript*—the official school record of the classes you took and the grades you received during your secondary education. Admissions offices will convert the grading system used in your country to an equivalent U.S. grade. If your grades are high, you will have a much better chance of entering a competitive university. If your grades are low, don't worry—there are still many opportunities for study in the United States! In any case, check on the availability of your transcripts or other academic records at an early stage so that you can have them sent to the U.S. schools in advance of your application deadlines.

Strength of Program

It is always best to apply to schools that offer strong programs in your field of study. But keep in mind that schools with good programs in a particular field are not always well-known universities. A small school with only undergraduate programs may offer an outstanding bachelor's degree curriculum in electrical engineering, yet not be well known internationally because it is not a research institution.

Don't make your selection based only on the reputation of the university. The outstanding reputations of Stanford, Harvard, and other well known universities are certainly deserved, but there are many other excellent schools as well. What matters is that you find the schools that are the most appropriate for you and your goals. In other words, finding the "best" school means finding the best school *for you*.

Real Advice from Real Students

1. Know why you are going to study in the United States, otherwise you'll struggle.

2. Focus your study as quickly as you can. It will simplify your research and decrease the amount of time you need to spend in school.

3. Get to know the professors in the programs that interest you.

4. Learn how to "sell yourself" in a substantial, credible way. It's perfectly acceptable in the United States to do this, and it is crucial for "getting ahead."

5. Make sure you're dedicated—it's a long and often difficult road to graduation.

Financial Resources

Check your financial resources against the actual costs for the colleges you have selected for application. Are your projections accurate, or do you need to make some adjustments to your financial goals?

PERSONAL CONSIDERATIONS

There are more than 3,300 accredited colleges and universities in the United States. With that kind of selection, you can have your choice of location, climate, campus size, and language preparation and academic orientation programs.

Location

Each of the 50 United States has different geography and characteristics. Some states, such as California, Texas, and Alaska, are very large and have a variety of climates and geographical traits. If you are interested in studying in a particular region of the country, try to locate colleges and universities in that region.

Are you familiar with the geography of the United States? Answer each question with *True* or *False*.

1. The United States has big cities and urban environments only in the East.
2. The United States has open spaces only in the Southwest.
3. The United States has warm weather and relaxed manners only in the South.
4. The United States has agriculture blended with industrial areas only in the Midwest.
5. The United States has scenic beauty only in the Rocky Mountain states and the Northwest.
6. The United States has good weather and "young" lifestyles only in the Southwest.

All of the statements above are *false*: Almost any combination of geography and culture can be found in most regions of the country. Most college catalogs have good descriptions of the regional and local environments of their campuses, so do some research on location before you decide.

Weather and Climate

How important is weather to you? If it is important, include climate and weather along with all the other factors when selecting your school.

Do you want to live in a climate similar to your home country or do you want to try something new? You may wish to experience four seasons, with cold, snowy winters and warm summers. On the other hand, you may wish to avoid the cold. Here's a rough description of the basic regions in the United States (not including the states of Hawaii and Alaska, of course!)

New England

States: *Connecticut, Maine, Massachusetts, New Hampshire, Rhode Island, Vermont*

The states in the far northeast of the United States are often called New England. Its largest city is Boston (Massachusetts). The region has a great deal of rural land and "wide open space," making it an attractive place for many outdoor and athletic vacationers. New England is famous for its beautiful geography, fishing villages, and historical sites.

Climate: Very cold in winter with a lot of snow; hot and mildly humid in summer.

Mid Atlantic

States: *Delaware, Maryland, New Jersey, New York, Pennsylvania*

A heavily populated area, the largest city in this region is New York City (New York). The region and people are extremely diverse.

Climate: Cold in winter; hot and very humid in summer.

South

States: *Alabama, Arkansas, Florida, Georgia, Kentucky, Louisiana, Mississippi, North Carolina, South Carolina, Tennessee, Virginia, West Virginia*

This area covers the coastline from the North Atlantic Ocean to the Gulf of Mexico. Atlanta (Georgia), and then Miami (Florida) are its largest cities.

Climate: Warm and sunny all year; subtropical; hurricanes and tornadoes can occur.

Midwest

States: *Illinois, Indiana, Iowa, Kansas, Michigan, Minnesota, Missouri, Nebraska, North Dakota, Ohio, South Dakota, Wisconsin*

The Midwest or "Great Plains" is the center of the country. Its geography is generally flat, with farmland that extends for miles and miles. Its largest cities are Chicago (Illinois) and Detroit (Michigan).

Climate: Extremely cold in winter; warm and pleasant in summer.

Rocky Mountains

States: *Colorado, Idaho, Montana, Nevada, Utah, Wyoming*

These states are home to the Rocky Mountains and a great many deserts and plains. Much of the region is lightly populated, with vast land areas undeveloped. Its largest cities are Denver (Colorado) and Las Vegas (Nevada).

Climate: Cold and snowy in winter; mild and warm in summer.

Southwest

States: *Arizona, New Mexico, Oklahoma, Texas*

Much of the land in these states is desert. The largest cities are Houston (Texas) and Phoenix (Arizona).

Climate: Very hot and dry in summer; mild in winter

Pacific Coast

States: *California, Oregon, Washington*

These states are know for their beauty and dramatic coastlines. It also produces most of the agricultural products of the United States. The largest cities are Los Angeles and San Diego (California). There are dense forests in the northern part of this region.

Climate: Sunny, mild weather all year, though there can be significant rainfall in Washington.

Language Preparation

You will need a high level of English proficiency in order to get the most out of your experience in the United States. You should be able to understand lectures, speak in class discussions, read textbooks, and write research papers.

If you are a graduate student, you will be competing with other students who have had a lot of experience preparing advanced research materials. Have you ever written a graduate level research paper? The experience can be difficult if you are not prepared.

Without strong language skills, you will not succeed. If your English is not as strong as you think it should be, enroll in a language program before you begin your academic study. Many students study English in the United States in special programs called *Intensive English Programs* or *IEPs*. In an IEP, you study English for 20 or more class hours each week, and for 10–15 hours outside of class. Kaplan, Inc. offers an excellent English and academic orientation program through its international programs. Contact Kaplan (refer to the international listing at the back of this book) for more information.

Do not leave your TOEFL examination to the last minute. If you are going to need additional English training, it is much better to know this information as early as possible.

Campus Size

American colleges and universities ranges in size from a few hundred students to over 40,000 students. A campus may be only a few buildings in a city or a very large piece of land that seems the size of a small city. The size of a campus and the number of students affect the atmosphere of a school, so you should consider this in your selection process.

Large schools (often state universities, such as the University of Illinois or the University of Texas) may offer the greatest number of fields of study and usually have large graduate programs. Their facilities (libraries, laboratories, theaters, etcetera) will be more extensive than those at smaller schools. Campus life may be more varied, with many activities available every day. On the other hand, classes there can be very large, and many lower-division classes can be taught by graduate students instead of professors.

A large or prestigious university may be a good choice for you if you want to attend a well-known school to be well-known in your home country, don't want to "stand out" in a crowd, or need specialized facilities for a particular field of study.

Smaller schools (often private, liberal arts schools, including those with very strong reputations, such as Oberlin College and Swarthmore College) may offer more personal attention, smaller classes and a quieter, less hurried atmosphere. On the other hand, smaller schools are usually more expensive than large state schools, and their facilities may be more limited. A smaller school may be a good choice if you want a less-crowded atmosphere and a lot of personal interaction with professors.

Academic Support

Most schools offer academic support programs (sometimes called *tutorial services*) for those who are having difficulty with a class. Sometimes, a student needs just a little extra assistance, particularly if she is a lower-division student taking general education classes. This kind of program may be especially important for international students who are trying to compete in a second or third language. Most academic support services are free. Do not hesitate to use them. If you think you have some areas of academic weakness, be certain the universities you choose offer academic support.

Campus Safety and Security

Many students (and their families) are worried about personal safety in the United States. Sometimes people in other countries think that the United States is a very violent country in which people are in danger every day.

Of course there is crime in America, just as there is crime in almost every country. Here, the level of violence is definitely higher than it should be. But the United States is generally a safe country for people who use common sense. Every big city in the world, including those considered very safe, has areas that are more dangerous than others, and those areas should be avoided.

Don't assume that the United States is really like a crime show on television! Most Americans live securely and go to work and to school without any fear or problems.

Most college and university campuses are like small cities. They generally have security offices that operate very much like police departments, and every college and university in the country has a program to reduce and control crime on campus. We know that some crime exists in any city, but on campuses in the United States, crime is seldom violent. Students must be careful, but an intelligent person is not likely to have any difficulty in keeping his or her possessions safe.

If you are particularly worried about crime and violence, you may wish to consider a school in an area that is relatively safe. Big cities usually have more crime problems than do small towns. The east and west coasts are often considered more dangerous than the interior parts of the country. Schools that are located in cities may be less safe than schools located in isolated rural settings. Feel free to bring up your concerns about safety with the admissions office before applying to a school. The issue of safety is a reality in this country, and people are accustomed to talking about it.

Sometimes a family member or friend has had a good experience at a particular school. While you should certainly consider this, you should not automatically choose the same school. Consider your own needs and goals.

USING YOUR RESOURCES

As you start to investigate your resources, you will realize that not all of them are available. Some of your former instructors may have moved, or the bookstore with the college references may be closed for a few days. No matter what obstacles you face, explore as many resources as you can. This effort will not be completed in a few days, so you will have plenty of time to complete your search at a later date.

Pick several schools that you would like to explore in some detail. As you proceed, you will become an expert in eliminating schools from your list. To narrow your list down:

1. Start with one criterion, such as your *field of study*. Start with 75–80 schools that have your field. Eliminate any schools that do not offer what you need at the appropriate level.

2. Next, apply another criterion. Perhaps financial resources is the next thing to consider. Of the schools that have your field of study, how many are financially realistic? Eliminate any schools that exceed your financial means.

3. Check on the average grades and test score results (such as SAT or GMAT) of the students admitted to the schools. The grading method will probably be unfamiliar to you, but you might be able to ask for a rough idea of the equivalent for your home country. Or, look at the percentages of students entering by class rank, which is often available to the public. Are you in the top 25% of your class? the top 50%? See how this fits with the schools that are left on your list. Note: Although you may be able to eliminate some schools on this basis, don't do this too drastically.

4. Now, examine the strength of the program. Although you won't have all the pertinent information, use what data is available. Keep only the strongest programs on your final list.

5. Next you will apply your own personal criteria. Spend a week or two doing this. Screen out enough schools so that you have a maximum of 30 schools or so. Once you reach this number, find out as much as you can about each school. Often, you will discover that a school that seemed to fit your needs at first actually does not. Eliminate more schools at this step.

Now you are ready to explore schools in depth.

Undergraduate Students

Go back and talk again with your secondary school guidance counselors. Now is the time for you to work really hard at looking up information about schools in their catalogs or on the Internet. Again, eliminate more schools. Notice how much your original list has been reduced! Now go over each remaining school with your adviser, noting advantages and disadvantages for each one. Finally, to complete this step, check the address (either email or regular mail) of the office of admission at each school still on your list. (By the way, it would be a good idea to make a photocopy of your list and keep it in a safe place. You have put in too much work to lose it now!)

Graduate Students

Your task is more complicated at this point than that of undergraduate students. While most undergraduate work in the United States is centered on classes, much of your work will be in research. You will take classes as well, but the professors will be working with you outside of your class-related activities. You will have an academic adviser who will closely supervise your study.

It is therefore very important that your interests in study and research match the professional interests of your professors. A master's degree program at one university can be quite different in content, emphasis, and philosophy than a program in the same field at a different university. Part of your selection process must be to find a good fit between your interests and the program you will enter.

Contact professors and others at your undergraduate university who are familiar with your work. If they are familiar with U.S. schools, they may be among the best resources you have. Get their suggestions and follow them up with guidance counselors at binational centers through the Fulbright Association if possible. If you are in an English program, discuss the recommendations with your adviser. Look at catalogs from as many schools that offer your field of study as possible. Keep eliminating schools from your list. However, if you find some interesting new possibilities, don't be afraid to add to your list of schools!

One useful way to check on your "fit" with graduate schools is to look at professional journals in your field. If you find articles that interest you, note the institutional affiliations of the authors. Give those schools special attention in your search. At the same time, if you notice articles that are definitely not interesting, note the same information about the authors' institutions and include it in your considerations.

Now look at your list once more. If it has more than 15 schools, cut the number down some more! If there are fewer than five, consider returning a few schools to the list (unless there are none that fit).

What to Check in a College Catalog or Website

❏ Location and campus setting

❏ Type of school (coed or single sex?)

❏ Size of student body

❏ Percentage of international students

❏ Academic calendar

❏ Academic support programs

❏ Student-faculty ratio

❏ Most popular majors

❏ On- and off-campus housing information

❏ Campus security provisions

❏ Admissions deadlines

❏ Application fees

❏ Required admissions tests and average score levels

❏ Tuition and fees

❏ Contact information/address and telephone

❏ Overall school profile

PLANNING YOUR TESTS

It's time to start applying to take the examinations that you will need in order to be admitted to the schools you have chosen. Depending on your situation, you may need such tests as TOEFL, SAT, GRE, GMAT, or LSAT. There are many other tests that might be required. If you are not sure of what you will need, be sure to read the application information that the colleges and universities will send you. That information will include the names of the tests that are required.

EVALUATING SCHOOL INFORMATION

After a reasonable time, you will receive information from the schools you contacted. If an important school does not respond, contact it again by email or fax and include a copy of your original request. Address your message to the director of international admissions.

Keep copies of all of your messages: If the school tells you later that it is too late to apply, you can document your attempts to get materials if you wish to ask for reconsideration.

If You Do Not Have Time to Complete All the Steps . . .

If you don't have enough time to do a thorough search, don't panic. You might want to get assistance from a commercial placement agency. If you do, it is critical to remain involved in the process. An experienced agency may be able to help you speed up the process, but do not limit your choices to the few schools that might have special relationships with the agency. It is very important to admissions officers that you make your own decisions. If someone else makes the decision for you, there is a good chance that you will regret this choice in time.

There are also advising services available in the United States that can be of assistance. If time is short, look carefully at options such as Kaplan's International Programs, which can provide you with advice and assistance in the application process as well as making English classes and orientation programs available as needed.

Read carefully all of the information that you have. On the basis of everything you have learned, you should be able to choose one or two schools that seem to meet your requirements and for which you seem qualified. We recommend that you also choose a school that may be slightly less competitive than your first choice but still offers a program you want and meets most of your criteria. This is often called a *safety school*. Finally, we suggest that you choose a school that is somewhat more selective than your first choice. This is a school that you would like to attend, but think that you probably would not be accepted. This is sometimes called a *stretch* or *reach school*.

Make sure that you understand the deadlines each school has. The deadlines will be different from one school to another. Some schools want you to submit an application by a certain date, but will continue to accept supporting documents (such as test scores and academic records) at a later time. Others will want everything to arrive at the same time. Make sure you use these deadlines in making your plans!

Check to see that you have registered for or taken all the exams required by your chosen schools. Some exam score results are valid for up to two years, while others must be taken close to the time of your application. Most schools will not look at your application until all of the required exam results and documentation have been received in your file, so make sure you arrange all of this early on.

After you check the deadlines and examination requirements, do a final check of your local resources. Take your selections back to your counselor, your professors, or your counseling center adviser. Ask them for their personal opinions on your choices.

Now you have made your selections and are ready to start the application process. Congratulations! Much of the time remaining in your time line will be taken up with waiting to hear from schools. Before schools make their admissions decisions, they have to wait for test results. You may also have filled out part of the application incorrectly, or may have omitted some important information, so you may be contacted by the admissions office.

The Admissions Process

State University of New York at Stony Brook

The Admissions Process | **5**

The first step in the admissions process is to obtain applications from the institutions at which you hope to study. Many application forms can be downloaded electronically directly from school websites. If that isn't possible, visit the educational section of the nearest U.S. consulate or write to or email the school admissions office. If you do write to the school, indicate the highest educational level you completed in your home country, and what field you wish to study. This is important, since the school may not offer the program you wish to study.

Once you have received the official applications, you are ready to begin the process. The first thing you should do is to make a notation of the application deadlines. Early February is typically when applications are due, though many schools have later deadlines for international applicants. Read your application carefully.

You might be asked to complete a preliminary application before a school will send you the official application. This is to determine your eligibility as based on your previous education, test scores, and financial resources available.

Applications require a great deal of information. Let's look at a few of the most common questions.

Read over your materials and make a list of what each university application requires.

1. What official records and transcripts do you need?
2. What documentation must you submit as proof of financial support?
3. Does the application require a statement of purpose (an explanation of *what* you want to pursue and *why*), or does it provide you with an assigned essay subject?
4. How many letters of reference or recommendation do you need?

Basic University Application Information

1. Biographical data
   - Name (If you are a married woman, include your maiden, or unmarried, name.)
   - Date and place of birth
   - Gender (male or female)
   - Current address (Is this different from your mailing address?)
   - Social Security number, if you have a nonimmigrant U.S. Social Security card
   - Marital status (single, married, divorced, or widowed)
   - Socioethnic background (This information is used by the university strictly for statistical purposes and does not affect your chance of being accepted.)

2. Education
   - Level of education you have completed
     —*Secondary school* (through grade 12 in the U.S. system)
     —*Undergraduate* (a two- or four-year degree)
     —*Graduate school* (master's, Ph.D., or equivalent)
   - Mailing addresses of your previous schools
   - Names of the principals and faculty chairmen at your previous schools

3. Personal References
   - Names, professional titles, and addresses of the people who will provide references for you (Most universities ask for three letters of reference, but this number can vary.)

4. Degree information
   - Level of education you are seeking
     —*Associate's degree*: A two-year degree program, either in a technical or vocational subject or in an academic, liberal arts program, typically completed at two-year *community colleges.*
     —*Bachelor's degree*: The first university degree (an undergraduate degree), typically completed in four years with a minimum of 120 semester credits.
     —*Master's degree*: The second university degree (a graduate degree), completed one to two years after a bachelor's degree.
     —*Doctorate*: The highest academic degree awarded (Medical Doctorate— M.D., Juris Doctorate—J.D., Doctor of Philosophy—Ph.D.)

5. What exams are required?

6. Does the school administer its own English proficiency exam?

7. Does the school require an interview?

8. If you are a performing arts student, is an audition required?

9. What is the application fee? How is it payable: money order, credit card, bank check? (Keep in mind that fees must be paid in U.S. dollars.)

Every school will want official records (or transcripts) from your previous schools. Most universities want to receive transcripts in English or accompanied by a certified English translation. Special exam results will also be required, such as British-pattern O-Levels and A-Levels, or licensing exams. It is very important to send a complete academic record: Some schools will deny admission if there is an unexplained gap in your academic history.

When you have made a list of all your official records, contact your previous schools to have them sent directly to the U.S. schools. Universities in the United States usually want to receive transcripts and exam results directly from "official institutions" rather than from you, the student. In general, schools will not accept official academic documents from you in any form, even if they are sealed.

Remember, it will probably take your previous schools a long time to mail out the required documents, so give them plenty of time. If you have not yet received an exam result or grades when you are ready to send your application, write that information on the application form. That way, the admissions office will know when it will receive the missing documents.

Graduate students must also send official records of all postsecondary (college-level) study. This means diplomas and degrees *as well as* quantitative evaluations of your previous course work and research. In many cases, this will be only a transcript of courses, dates, and marks received that is sent directly from the previous university to the school. If your previous work involved research, the admissions office may want an abstract or copy of that work.

ADMISSIONS EVALUATION

There is a fundamental difference between undergraduate and graduate admissions evaluation. Undergraduate admissions are processed by the university office of admissions. In general, graduate admissions decisions are made by faculty committees within the academic department to which you are applying. The graduate admissions process is much more time-consuming than the undergraduate process. In both cases, it is essential that you observe the admissions materials deadlines.

FINANCIAL DOCUMENTATION

Each school will need to receive official documentation of your financial resources. This is to ensure that you are prepared to meet the costs of your education. Documentation of financial resources can take many forms.

1. A completed *financial information form* (if one is included with your application). This form must be *personally* signed by you and your parent or sponsor providing your financial support. That means no photocopies!

2. A *certified bank statement* that proves that you or your sponsor has sufficient funds to support your education and living costs. Most banks are familiar with this form. If you are not certain that you have the correct form, contact the admissions office and ask for specific details.

3. If you will be receiving a scholarship or support from a government, organization, or business, provide a *letter from the sponsoring agency* confirming the receipt and amount of that portion of your financial support.

4 If you will be sponsored by someone in the United States, an *affidavit of support* is required from the U.S. Department of Education. If needed, you can obtain a blank copy of this form from the school to which you are applying.

Don't forget to:

1. *Photocopy all your applications*
2. *Have a good filing system for your application documents, and use it*
3. *Contact a school if there is a question you cannot answer*
4. *Ask someone with a good eye for detail to proofread your final-draft application*
5. *Put your name on all pages, including all pages of your essay, in case they are misplaced*

APPLICATION ESSAY OR STATEMENT OF PURPOSE

Almost all application forms require that you write some type of essay. A few schools provide you with an assigned topic on which you must write, yet most schools ask you to prepare a *statement of purpose* in which you state your reasons for wanting to study at that particular university. The admissions packet may contain a special form, or it may simply provide directions regarding the content and length of your essay.

Following are some examples of what you might be asked to write.

1. Please write a detailed, accurate statement of your academic and professional goals, why you wish to study in the United States, and why you have chosen ABC College.

2. On additional paper, write an essay on one of the following topics. Your essay should be one to two pages in length and typed or neatly printed. Your essay will give us more insight into your personality and interests and will serve as a writing sample.

   a. Words can evoke vivid memories, powerful feelings, or a sense of excitement. What is your favorite word and why?

   b. If you could spend a day with any person, living or dead, or a literary character, with whom would it be? What would you do or discuss?

   c. Tell us about your academic, personal, or professional goals and describe how they have or have not changed over time.

3. Select and describe those experiences and relationships in your background which you feel are significant in your development as a person. What connections can you make between those experiences and your plans for graduate study and future career?

The essay is a very serious portion of your application, so be sure to give yourself plenty of time to work on it. The essay is your opportunity to tell the admissions officers what makes you special. Don't tell them how wonderful their institution is. Instead, give them some background on you which illustrates why the university is the best choice for you. Things to consider including in your essay:

1. Academic strengths

2. Personal interests

3. Role models (people whom you greatly admire) that have influenced your choices

Once you have completed your essay, make sure to edit it carefully. Ask a friend to review it (preferably a native English speaker). If your goals seems unfocused or unrelated to the program, rewrite the essay. It's okay to write your essay over several times: Most successful writers commonly write drafts before coming up with a final product. Check your spelling and your grammar. Show the admissions committee how strong your English skills are!

For undergraduate students, the goal of the essay is to give the admissions office some understanding of how well you match with the characteristics of its program.

Here are a few questions to ask yourself before you begin writing:

1. Why did you select this university? Provide details and examples of how the university can help you reach your educational goals.

2. What, specifically, about the curriculum in your major field of study appeals to you? Is it the courses offered, internship of research opportunities, faculty members?

3. What are you able to contribute to the university? Explain a little about your background. As an international student, you are in a unique position to bring diversity to the college campus. Do you have any special experience or qualification that the admissions officer might want to know?

It is acceptable to say positive things about yourself in the United States as long as you don't boast (exaggerate). If there is something about yourself that you would like to include, be sure to do so, as long as it is pertinent to the essay!

For graduate students, the essay has another purpose. When you write an essay for graduate school, you are trying to convince faculty members that *they* would like to work with *you* over the next several years. If you can convince them that your professional goals are consistent with the mission of their department, you will have a much better chance of acceptance. In a graduate essay, then, it is very important to include your experience and background in the area of study you have chosen. Explain your motivation in terms of why you chose this field, what your long-term goals are, and how the school can help you to reach them.

LETTERS OF RECOMMENDATION

Most applications will ask for three letters of recommendation. A *letter of recommendation* is written by someone who knows you well, such as a teacher, an employer, or a professional who has supervised you. This person will communicate (in writing) that you are gifted and capable of contributing to the institution if you are accepted.

Whom *you ask to write your personal recommendation can impact how you are perceived as an applicant.*

Some application packets will provide forms with instructions, while others will simply provide instructions. Follow the directions provided for each: Some schools require that you have recommendations sent directly to them, while others allow you to include them in sealed (closed and private) envelopes along with your other application materials.

Your recommendations should be specific to the institution to which you are applying. An old, photocopied letter stating that you are a good student is not acceptable. A strong recommendation letter should be written with one university in mind. The writer should provide as many personal details as possible. Vague generalities should be avoided: Admissions officers want to know that the people recommending you know you well and support your academic success.

Graduate recommendations are *very* important. Undergraduate recommendations are read in an attempt to assess the student's potential. Graduate recommendations, on the other hand, are read to see how a student would fit in with the professional interests of the faculty members. These letters should be written from one professional colleague to another. They should discuss your professional and academic achievements in addition to your potential.

EXAMS AND DEADLINES

The application form will list the exams that are required for a particular university. If you have not already taken them, do so without delay. Your exam scores must be evaluated by the admissions office before your application will be complete.

The following standardized examinations are common for American colleges and graduate schools:

SAT Exam

This is an undergraduate admissions test. There are two types of SAT, but the SAT I alone is the most common test for undergraduate admissions.

SAT I Reasoning Test: measures verbal and mathematical reasoning abilities

SAT II Subject Tests: a series of 22 tests that measure knowledge of a particular subject. There are five general subject areas: English, history and social studies, mathematics, sciences, and languages.

Graduate Record Exam (GRE)

This is a computer-based graduate admissions test. It is not administered with paper and pencil. The test is very easy to conduct, so don't worry if you are not very comfortable using a computer. You will simply be "clicking" your answers with the electronic mouse.

The *General Test* measures verbal, mathematical, and analytical concepts that have been acquired over a long period of time. The *Subject Tests* are more specialized exams that test knowledge of specific subject areas (i.e., psychology, biology, etcetera). Most graduate programs require scores for the General Test or a Subject Test—or both.

Law School Admissions Test (LSAT)

The LSAT is required for admission to all law schools. The LSAT measures skills that are considered essential for success in law: comprehending complex written material; analyzing arguments and drawing reliable conclusions; organizing information; and writing persuasively.

Medical College Admissions Test (MCAT)

The MCAT is required for admission to most medical schools. Although the MCAT is both a skills-based and a knowledge-based exam, it places special emphasis on analytical reasoning, abstract thinking, and problem solving.

Graduate Management Admissions Test (GMAT)

Most graduate business and management programs require submission of GMAT scores. The test assesses skills relevant to graduate studies in business and management, measuring basic verbal, quantitative, and writing skills.

Test of English as a Foreign Language (TOEFL)

The TOEFL tests the ability to understand North American English. It was developed to help American and Canadian colleges and universities evaluate the level of English language proficiency of the international students who apply. The content of the TOEFL includes listening comprehension, reading comprehension, and structure and written expression.

THE ACADEMIC CALENDAR

Most universities follow one of two schedule systems.

Semester System: For those schools that follow the semester system, there are two semesters, each lasting 16–18 weeks. The first semester is called the fall term (from September to December), and the second semester is the winter or spring term (from January to May or June).

Quarter System: For those schools that follow this system, there are three "quarters" in an academic year, each 10 or 11 weeks. The three quarters (or terms) are usually referred to as the fall, winter, and spring terms.

EVALUATION OF YOUR FOREIGN CREDENTIALS

It is possible you will be asked by an American school to have your credentials evaluated by an external foreign credential service. *Credentials* are documents that represent your educational background: official diplomas, degrees, exam results, and transcripts for courses completed. Some schools do not have the resources to evaluate foreign documents themselves, and so they enlist the help of outside professionals. Be advised that there is a fee for this service.

A credential service will examine your documents for accuracy and authenticity. You will then be informed as to whether your credentials are equivalent to those in the United States. The following items will be converted into U.S. semester credit hours: units completed, grades, class hours, length of course, and hours of study.

Evaluation agencies do not make admission decisions. They are only part of the process in applying and getting accepted to a school in the United States.

Keep in mind that many large schools are accustomed to evaluating foreign documents themselves, so this type of service may not be necessary. If you are asked to use a foreign credential service, the university will provide you names and contact information, and possible, an application form. Do not contact a credential service yourself before the university has asked you to do so. At that time, you will need to complete the application and submit the appropriate documents required. Once all proper documentation is received, it takes approximately four weeks to process your credentials.

The national association that oversees the individual credential services is called the *National Association of Credential Evaluation Services* (NACES). NACES member organizations are experienced professionals who conduct research, have expertise in foreign educational systems, institutions, programs and educational documents from outside the United States.

You should send all official diplomas, degrees, examination results, and transcripts for studies completed, beginning with the end of secondary school. An ***official document*** is the original document in the original language. Official transcripts may be issued in English and contained in a sealed envelope. A photocopy is not acceptable.

If you have only one original of your academic documents, you must certify and notarize any photocopies. Make sure that you copy all pages, front and back. Once you have been admitted to the university, you will be expected to bring the original documents for review by the admissions office. These documents will be returned to you.

If your original credentials are not in English, submit the original documents along with a certified translation. University officials and evaluation services will not work with translations alone. The translation must be signed by a notary indicating who provided the translation.

Credential evaluators review the level of study completed (secondary or postsecondary) in the context of the educational system. They consider where the final degree leads to in the home country, the purpose and intent of the program, whether the courses are offered at a university or another institution, and whether the studies lead to a higher level of academic study or into the job market. This is important in making equivalency determinations. Once again, this is also where the educational ladder plays an important part in the evaluation process.

Evaluators review the material that was covered and the scope of the program to determine whether it was vocational, technical or academic in nature. They also review the status of the school you attended in your home country; noting if it is recognized by the Ministry of Education, the Council of Higher Education, or the official recognition body of your home country.

Evaluators also assess the number of years of schooling you completed, as represented by the documents submitted and the complexity of the program completed. This may involve a syllabus review.

What if the credentials presented are results of a performance on a national examination? Some schools will indicate in the application which secondary level certificates or national examinations they will allow for advanced standing credit, such as the German Abitur, the Italian Maturitá, or the Hong Kong GCE Advanced Levels. Each school is different, so you must review the materials you receive from the school carefully to find this information. By receiving advanced standing, you will be exempted from coursework required for the degree program you wish to enroll.

If you have completed studies that are postsecondary, or beyond the secondary (high) school level, you may be eligible for an exemption of courses towards the degree program in the United States. This is referred to as *transfer credit*. This is credit given for courses that apply toward the degree program requirements and have been successfully passed with a minimum grade of C or better (in United States terms). Accepting the minimum grade of C may vary, depending on the individual policy of the institution you are applying to. These studies must also be completed at a recognized institution in your home country. Some schools may provide you with an exemption from required courses based on previous studies completed. The admissions officer in the United States will make the determination and recommendation of the transfer credit courses awarded.

Students applying to American universities for a graduate degree must have a bachelor's degree from the United States or the equivalent. The credential evaluator will make an assessment of your educational background to determine if the degree you hold is equivalent.

Your previous academic performance or quality (in other words, *grades*) also will be assessed. In the United States, grades for completed coursework are generally a continual assessment throughout the semester of the class. In other countries, grades may not be assessed or determined until the end of the course and the examination.

Schools may ask on the application for a self-reported **GPA**, which stands for *grade point average*. In the United States, most schools grade courses on a letter scale with a corresponding numerical scale as follows:

$$A = 4.0 \quad B = 3.0 \quad C = 2.0 \quad D = 1.0 \quad F = 0.0$$

Grades are an indicator of the quality of work that a student has completed. In the United States, students must have a minimum GPA of 2.0 to graduate at the undergraduate level and a 3.0 to graduate at the master's graduate level.

The grading scale in your country will likely be different from the one used in the United States. So when the application asks for a GPA, leave it blank or write in the grade you received in your country. For example, a 4.0 grading scale is used in

Thailand, and a numerical final grade is given. This is also true for India and the United Kingdom, where the final degree is classified as First Division, Second Class Honours, etcetera. Indicate this grade in that question.

YOUR CHANCES FOR ADMISSION

Once the assessment is completed, you will be notified in writing of your acceptance to the schools you applied to. If you have done a good job in your selection process, you should be fairly certain of admittance to at least one or two schools. As we mentioned in chapter 4, you should apply to at least one *safety school*, meaning a school at which you will almost certainly be accepted. This works better for undergraduates than graduates, but it never hurts to be safe.

While smaller schools may give you a fast response if you are an undergraduate, it is likely that larger schools (and all graduate programs) will take several months to reply. This is true for American students as well. Remember that a large university may have to process more than 100,000 detailed applications each year. There may be as many as 20,000 applications from international students, each requiring careful examination and professional evaluation of qualifications from hundreds of different educational systems. It is not surprising that the notifications take a long time! Be patient.

Colleges put some applicants on a waiting list in case they have underestimated the number of admitted students who will actually enroll. Wait-listed students are given the opportunity to fill any empty slots.

It may be smart to make travel reservations before you hear about your acceptance, particularly if you are confident that you will be accepted at your first choice school. If the school takes a long time to notify you, it may be difficult to make air travel reservations at a late date. Every year, hundreds of international students are unable to come to the United States to study because of this. Make your plans in advance.

A few weeks after you submit your applications, contact your selected universities to be certain that all materials have been received. If a university has not responded after two or three months, don't be afraid to call or email to ask about the status of your application. A little added interest in the institution will only improve your chances.

Special Programs and Opportunities

Indiana University/Bloomington

Special Programs and Opportunities

ADVANCED PROGRAMS FOR SCHOLARS AND POSTDOCTORAL FELLOWS

If you have completed doctoral study but are not a faculty member at a university, there are many programs designed for further teaching or research.

Scholars-in-Residence and Visiting Scholars

There are hundreds of programs that give outstanding scholars the opportunity to spend time at a U.S. university or other research location such as the Smithsonian Institution in Washington, D.C. In most situations, a scholar will be expected to lecture on her field of specialization or to do specific research (or both). In some cases, a scholar will be invited by an institution, but most of the time, such opportunities are advertised in professional and government publications and on the Internet. Most programs are open to international scholars, though there will be domestic competition as well. The time frame for visiting scholars is from one day to several months, while scholars-in-residence may stay from a few weeks to two years.

In some cases, the support of the institution is limited to providing facilities for research, but in most cases, a stipend and living allowance are also provided as a condition of the visit or residency. It is important to understand any conditions that might come with a program before accepting this type of position.

One of the best-known and largest of the scholarly programs designed primarily for international exchange is the *Fulbright Scholar-in-Residence* program. For details, contact the binational Fulbright Commission in your country. Website: http://exchanges.state.gov/education/commiss.htm.

Lecturers

In many respects, visiting lecturers have opportunities similar to those of visiting scholars and the same sources of information generally apply. The main difference is that lecturers are usually expected to remain at an academic location for a very limited period and are not expected to do research. Visiting lectureships are often easier to obtain, as they involve much less commitment on the part of the receiving institution or organization.

Dissertation Fellowships

There are small numbers of fellowships available for those doctoral candidates who have completed all course work but have not yet submitted a dissertation. If the dissertation topic is considered very important and the candidate has strong faculty sponsorship, he might be awarded a dissertation fellowship. This kind of financial support is limited and is intended to allow for the completion of the dissertation. It is distinct from the postdoctoral fellowship discussed below.

Postdoctoral Fellowships

Postdoctoral fellowships are a major source of research funding for those who have completed their basic scholarly training and are interested in periods of advanced research. Unlike visiting scholars, postdoctoral fellows have not yet established their academic reputations, but are in the process of building their careers.

There are thousands of postdoctoral fellowships available. Many are sponsored by or administered through large organizations such as the Fulbright Foundation, the Ford Foundation, and the Institute of International Education. Many others are offered directly by universities and research institutions, both public and private.

As fellowships and other grants are continually changing, it is important that junior faculty members and those completing doctoral studies stay current about available opportunities. There is probably no better way to do this than the Internet. If you do not have Internet access, check with a university research facility or library in your country.

Two comprehensive websites for fellowship and grant resources are:

International Funding Sources
This site, run by the University of Iowa, lists hundreds of funding sources. It has direct links to contact sites.
Website: http://www.uiowa.edu/~vpr/research/sources/intfund.htm

Middlebury College
The Grants Office at Middlebury College has a comprehensive database of funding sources, including foundation and university grants.
Website: http://www.middlebury.edu/~grants/linksandforms2.html

SUMMER PROGRAMS

There are two kinds of summer programs available: recreational (summer camp), and educational (summer study).

Summer Camp

The tradition of summer camp is very strong in the United States: For the summer months of July and/or August, children attend a full-time recreational or educational program. While some programs accept individuals up to 25 years old, most programs are intended for those between the ages of 6 and 18.

There are many types of camps: Some camps are located in rural wilderness sites near lakes, while other are on school campuses. Some camps are "all boys" or "all girls"; others are co-ed (for boys and girls). Some camps are full-time residential programs, while others are day programs in which campers return home at night.

General camps combine activities such as nature studies, sports, hiking, camping, and swimming, Academic camps focus on one academic area, such as science. Sports camps concentrate on the development of athletic skills. Arts camps focus on performing, creative, and fine arts. And travel camps provide campers with travel and cultural experiences.

Many international students choose to work as staff counselors at these camps. This experience is an excellent way to become familiar with the American way of life.

American Camping Association
This association has extensive information for international students looking for summer employment. The ACA establishes standards for camps and has an accreditation program for approved camps.
Website: http://www.acacamps.org/jobs.htm

Another useful resource is the book *Yale Daily News Guide to Summer Programs*, available through English language bookstores. The book gives details about many types of summer programs.

Summer Study

Many academic institutions offer summer terms. If you need to take a class as preparation for a higher-level class offered during the regular term, summer study may be useful. Although schools tend to offer a smaller selection of classes in the summer, they usually include basic subjects that are foundations for more advanced work.

Suppose an undergraduate engineering student needs to take calculus before starting scientific physics. She also needs a class in precalculus because she isn't familiar with the system of mathematical notation and proof in the United States. If she waits to take precalculus in the fall semester, she will not be ready for scientific physics in the spring. Her academic progress could be subject to considerable delays, which can be expensive. If she takes precalculus in the summer, however, she would be ready to take calculus in the normal sequence and would save time and money in the long run.

Intensive English preparation is another way you can spend your summer. Moving from university preparatory ESL directly into a degree program can make the transition to study in a United States school much easier for you.

Finally, some students take summer courses to accelerate their degree programs. While this does not work in all fields, an outstanding student might be able to reduce his stay in a university degree program by up to six months. This can be very important in terms of financial resources. Before you pursue this option, check with your international student advisor to see whether it is appropriate for your situation.

SHORT-TERM TRAINING AND INTERNSHIPS

Training programs from one day up to six months in length are called short-term. These are not typically programs that lead to academic degrees, though they may carry academic credit. They are generally designed to achieve a specific objective: learning a new computer language, perhaps, or teaching a group of traffic control supervisors the latest in traffic management techniques. There are many kinds of institutions that offer such programs:

Extension Programs

Many schools have branches called extension programs. These programs offer courses outside the regular university curriculum. You may be familiar with the idea of extension programs if you have considered studying English as a second language in the United States; many intensive ESL programs are offered through university extension divisions.

Extension divisions are organized so that they can create short-term programs to meet a specific demand. For example, if the Ministry of Agriculture in Japan wanted to train its agricultural health and safety standard trainees in English, the Japanese government might request that a university extension program assemble an English course. The university would negotiate a training contract with the foreign government and then develop and teach the course.

Private Companies

Private companies also offer training courses in their areas of expertise. A computer manufacturing company might offer classes for technicians from purchasing companies, teaching them how to perform maintenance on the newest equipment. A financial services company might teach classes on basic investment and retirement planning.

Opportunities Sponsored by the U.S. Government

There is a division of the U.S. government called The Graduate School of the U.S. Department of Agriculture. It teaches a wide variety of short-term, career-related programs intended for domestic and international audiences. These may be available for individual enrollment, though they are usually designed for specific target groups. Instructors are drawn from government, business and academia. For more information, contact:

USDA Graduate School
Website: http://grad.usda.gov/
Email: pubaffairs@grad.usda.gov

Community Colleges

Many community colleges offer short-term, nonacademic training courses, primarily in vocational fields or in areas of personal development. You could enroll in all types of course, ranging from secretarial skills to computer data entry to nature photography to local history. Short-term training institutions are easily found on the Internet. Do a search on the Web using the keywords "short-term training."

FOR STUDENTS WITH DISABILITIES

International students are often surprised at the American emphasis on equal educational opportunities for students with physical, developmental, and learning disabilities. Systems have been implemented to allow a student with disabilities to study and complete his education in the same manner as one without disabilities. While not every situation is possible, there are many opportunities open to international students with disabilities.

In higher education, there are a few key resources for disabled international students:

HEATH Resource Center
This division of the American Council on Education is an information exchange on postsecondary education for individuals with disabilities.
Phone: (202) 939-9320
Website: http://www.HEATH-resource-center.org/
Email: heath@ace.nche.edu

Mobility International
This non-profit organization connects people with disabilities from all over the world. It has extensive resources for international students.
Phone: (541) 343-1284
Website: http://www.miusa.org
Email: info@miusa.org

Almost all U.S. schools have some provision for facilitating the education of students with disabilities. If you have a disability and are interested in studying in the United States, do the same kind of college search described in earlier chapters. Once you have decided on the appropriate academic environment, contact the admissions office and ask about services available for disabled students.

In some ways, the most sophisticated systems of support are to be found in the two-year community colleges in the United States. These schools have long traditions of providing many types of educational opportunities in their local communities. They often have very strong guidance, evaluation, special support, and academic programs designed to maximize educational opportunities. If you are looking for a starting point, you should consult an educational counselor and consider an appropriate two-year school.

INTENSIVE ENGLISH PROGRAMS (IEPS)

With over 500 full-time IEPs in the United States, you are probably overwhelmed by the possibilities for English language study. Most IEPs endorse the TESOL Core Standards for Postsecondary Programs. TESOL (Teachers of English to Speakers of Other Languages) developed these standards to ensure quality ESL instruction. The American Association of Intensive English Programs (AAIEP) has also developed guidelines for IEPs.

For information on specific programs, go to:

Commission on English Language Program Accreditation
This is a non-profit corporation that accredits programs in English language.
Its website lists all accredited programs across the country.
Website: http://www.cea-accredit.org/

The American Association of Intensive English Programs
The AAIEP website provides an extremely detailed program description of IEPs around the country. It includes detailed costs, class size, and class description.
Website: http://www.aaiep.org

Your choice to study English in the United States involves a large commitment. Here are some tips to help you select the right program:

1. Decide where in the United States you would like to study. If you plan on attending university following the program, you will probably want to study English in the same region.

2. Gather information. Is the IEP affiliated with a university? A program is not necessarily better or worse because it is affiliated with a university. Can you receive academic credit? What is the average class size? Smaller is better, but a very small program may not have all the levels of instruction that a larger program has, nor all the support services.

3. Consider the cost. Costs for IEPs can vary widely. It is quite possible to find a program that has quality instruction at a reasonable price. In addition to the differences in program price, you must also consider the cost of living in the city you choose. In the large cities of the Northeast, food and housing costs will be higher than in a small town in the Midwest.

4. Be careful when you read informational brochures with beautiful pictures! Most brochures are written with the intention of "selling" you a program. Read all literature carefully and try to cross-reference a program with another source. Try to speak with students who have attended the program you are considering. Ask American citizens if they have heard of the program or the university and what their opinion is. The more sources of information, the better for you.

Chances are you will have a rewarding experience at whatever IEP you choose because the vast majority of programs strive for excellence of instruction and service. But consider your personal and career goals when shopping around for a program. Be careful of advertising sales strategies by educating yourself. And be sure to avoid large groups of people who speak your own language! Otherwise, you will never get the change to put into practice what you learn.

Preparation for Studying in the United States

Lafayette University

Preparation for Studying in the United States

Now that you have been admitted to the program of your choice, it is time to address the steps you must take to go to the United States. You will need to communicate with your new school, obtain a student visa, make housing and financial plans, discuss insurance issues, and create a prearrival checklist.

VISA PREPARATION

While you are in the United States you are considered a nonimmigrant. A **nonimmigrant** is an alien in the United States who has a distinct goal. When that goal is achieved, the nonimmigrant returns home. There are approximately 50 classifications of nonimmigrant status. Some of them are listed here.

Tourist Visas

If you are still unsure about studying in the United States and are still making a final decision, it is possible to visit prospective schools without receiving an F-1 visa stamp. If you have the financial resources to take a short visit to the United States, here are a few options.

Visa Waiver Status

If you are a citizen of one of the countries listed below, you can enter the United States for 90 days or less without obtaining a U.S. visa. Instead, you can obtain Visa Waiver Program (VWP) status. There are no extensions of stay for longer than 90 days.

To enter the United States on VWP, you must have a valid passport and must be a citizen (not simply a resident) of the participating country. You must have a round-trip transportation ticket. And you must have proof of finances and a completed visa waiver arrival/departure form (Form I-94W), in which you waive the right to a hearing of exclusion or deportation. This form can be obtained from travel agents and at ports of entry.

Important Note: If you enter the country on VWP status, you will not be allowed to change or extend your nonimmigrant status while in the United States. In other words, you cannot change to F-1 or J-1 status. You must exit the country and re-enter with an F-1 or J-1 visa.

Visa Waiver Program: Participating Countries

Andorra	Iceland	Portugal
Argentina	Ireland	San Marino
Austria	Italy	Singapore
Australia	Japan	Slovenia
Belgium	Liechtenstein	Spain
Brunei	Luxembourg	Sweden
Denmark	Monaco	Switzerland
Finland	The Netherlands	the United Kindgom
France	New Zealand	Uruguay
Germany	Norway	

B-2 Tourist Visa Status

If you are not eligible for the VWP program but you still wish to take a short trip to the United States, you can apply for a B-2 tourist visa. With a B-2 visa, you will be allowed to stay for three months, and can apply for an extension of an additional three months, or apply for a change of status. If you do plan to extend your B-2 visa, the extension application be received at INS before the date of expiration of your current status (as indicated on your I-94).

Changing from B to F visa status is a tricky proposition. A B visa is for doing "touristy" things and never study or work. Entering the country on a B tourist visa with the intent of changing your status once you have entered the country is misrepresentation and is therefore illegal. The consequences for this can be quite severe.

Even though Waiver Treaty status and B-2 visa status may appear to be convenient, many international student advisors do not recommend them to prospective students because of the serious risks involved.

Did You Know the Following Facts?

1. If you enter the United States under the Visa Waiver Program as a tourist, you may stay for up to 90 days. This cannot be changed or extended.

2. If you overstay your legal authorized time in the United States by more than 180 days but less than one year will be barred from re-entering the United States for three years. If you overstay your legal authorized time by one year, you will be barred for ten years.

3. Your monthly rent (for your residence) will be approximately 25–33% of your total monthly expenses. It is by far the largest expense college students have after tuition.

4. Medical insurance is very important because the United States does not have a national health program or social medical care. Medical care is very expensive.

If you wish to enter the United States without obtaining an F-1 visa, or have no intention of returning home before studies begin, you can apply for a B-2 prospective student visa. In order to obtain this visa, you must indicate your academic intentions and demonstrate financial support to a United States Consul. Even though it is not required, presenting your admissions letter will increase the chances of getting it approved. If you are successful and are able to enter the United States, contact your prospective student advisor for an application for change of status immediately.

Student Visas

Here are a few of the visas that are designed for students.

F-1 status: for full-time students at an academic or language institution

J-1 status: for exchange visitors (this status may require you to spend two years in your home country after you finish your U.S. studies)

M-1 status: for students at a vocational or nonacademic institution

Since F–1 status is for full-time students, it will be discussed at length here.

F-1 Status

F–1 status is for students pursuing full-time studies at an academic or language institution. Following is a list of things you should do in order to secure an F-1 visa.

1. Find out if your chosen school is eligible to accept and register F-1 students. The best way to find out this information is to read the college catalog. Look at the general procedures section *and* the international students section.

Be sure to also read the section for American students. That section might have important information for *all* students, domestic and international. If you receive your admission letter and you have not been given instructions on how to obtain a F-1 visa, call your admissions office immediately.

2. After you have been admitted to a qualified school, you must obtain an I-20 document in order to be issued an F-1 visa. Though each school has a different process, the basic legal requirements are the same. The ***Designated School Official*** (DSO) will issue you an I-20 document once it is determined that you have met all the requirements (or *standards*) for admission: academic requirements, language proficiency, enrollment in a full course of study, financial certification, and in some cases, proof of prior education related to chosen field of study.

The DSO can be found in the admissions office, the registrar's office, or the international student office. Unless you have been instructed differently, all of your immigration questions should be addressed to the DSO who signed your I-20. Immigration laws and regulations are very complex, and you should not receive advice on this topic from your family, friends, U.S. government offices, teachers, or lawyers before you have asked your DSO these questions.

When you receive your I-20, you will notice it has two pages. The top page is called the *I-20 School copy* and the bottom page, the *I-20 ID (student) copy*. Review this document for accuracy. Make sure your name, birth date, country of your birth, citizenship, your financial sponsorship, and your degree level are correct. Also, make sure it was signed by your DSO. If you have any questions, contact your school. If everything is correct and you have a valid passport, you are ready to apply for your F-1 visa stamp.

You will see many dates on your I-20; your birth date, you school's approval date, completion date, and date issued. It is important that you look at the *reporting* date that appears in section 5. This is the "no later than" date when you are expected to

---

Did You Know the Following Facts?

1. You can enter the United States up to 90 days prior to your university start date.

2. If you miss your start date and show up a couple of days late, you might not have a problem at your entry port. But if you're a week late (or more), you might be denied entry. As a safety precaution, notify the I-20 granting institution and ask for a late-entry letter. This is a document from the school acknowledging that late entry is acceptable.

---

arrive at your school. So plan accordingly. Specifically, complete all applications in such a way that you can receive your I-20 at least a month before start date, given that most consular offices prefer meetings by appointment, and getting an appointment time can be difficult.

Each United States consulate and embassy around the world has a certain process for applying for visas. Be sure to contact the post to which you will present your application. You can expect to be asked for the following items:

- A valid passport (except for Canadians)
- A certificate of eligibility (an I-20 form and F-1)
- Financial documentation (usually the same documentation you presented to your school in order to obtain your I-20)

Another very important requirement of your application will be your ability to prove to consul that you have a permanent residence outside the United States and that you intend to return to your home when you complete your degree.

Visa Denial

The most popular reason for visa denial to students is the designation "not qualified under Section 214(b) of the Immigration and Nationality Act." This section states: "Every alien shall be presumed to be an immigrant until he establishes to the satisfaction of the consular officer, at the time of the application for a visa, and the immigration officers, at the time of the application for admission, that he is entitled to a nonimmigrant status . . . ." To avoid this situation, be ready to present proof of employment, real estate, and family bank accounts based in your home country. These are considered as personal and social aspects having "ties" to your home country.

If you are denied a visa based on 214(b), usually your ISA, DSO or American supporters cannot help you. All evidence to counteract this decision comes from your home country resources. For more information you can request the Department of State Publication 9772 from the Bureau of Consular Affairs at the United States Department of State, and notify your ISA. This publication is designed for students entering the United States for the first time. However, if you have visited and stayed in this country before, the following information may also be helpful.

Those who have visited and stayed in the United States after September 1996 should be aware of three sections of a new federal law called *Illegal Immigration Reform and Immigrant Responsibility Act (IIRIRA)*. What follows is the language of those three sections and an explanation of how they effect you.

The Effect of the IIRIRA on Nonimmigrant Status

1. Foreign students in Public Elementary, Secondary, and Adult Education Programs Run by Secondary Schools, Section 346, which states, as of November 30, 1996:

   - No elementary or adult education students may obtain F-1 status to attend publicly funded schools and/or programs.
   - Public high school students obtaining F-1 status are limited to 12 months.

   Students violating this section are barred from the United States for five years.

2. Elimination of Consulate Shopping for Visa Overstayers, Section 632, which states, as of September 30, 1996:

   - Nonimmigrants remaining in the United States beyond the period of authorized stay have their current visa stamps voided and may only apply for new visa stamps in their country of nationality or permanent residence.

3. Aliens Unlawfully Present, Section 641, which states, as of April 1, 1997:
   - Aliens accumulating at least 180 days (but less than one year) of unlawful presence starting this date will be refused re-entry to the United States for three years
   - Aliens accumulating one year or more of unlawful presence starting with this date will be refused entry to the United States for 10 years.

The impact of any section of this law on your plans could be great. If you believe any of the information above applies to you, you should contact your school's DSO for his or her advice immediately.

But remember, think positively. The great majority of student applications for F-1 visas are approved.

At this time, you have received your I-20 and F-1 visa through contacts with the admissions and international students advisor's office at your new school. Now you will begin to be acquainted to other types of offices such as the bursar's office, registrar's office, and housing office.

TRANSFER OF FUNDS

Your school might expect you to be prepared to pay your entire term's tuition at the time of registration. Since you are not advised to carry this much money with you in person, it is advisable to electronically transfer (or wire) these funds to your school's account before you arrive at the school.

In many countries, it is difficult to transfer funds in enough time to meet your school's deadlines. Contact your international student advisor's office or bursar's office to get instructions about transferring your funds. Usually, you need a copy of your tuition bill. The bursar's office will give you the necessary bank account numbers to make your deposit.

Many foreign banks will allow you to use your I-20 to determine the exact amount available to be transferred from your home country. Many schools use a document called a *Monetary Exchange Form*. This form reflects your tuition, service fees, living, and other miscellaneous costs and your prospective financial sponsors. If you are not able to transfer money to your school before you arrive, ask about other services, such as fifty-fifty payment or deferment plans.

Again, you are strongly advised not to bring your tuition fees in cash or in traveler's checks. The only funds to bring in this fashion are your *"start-up" funds*—money you will need for initial costs in the United States. We recommend that you bring about $500 for this purpose. The balance of your start-up money should be in traveler checks or transferred to your personal bank account.

"Start-up" costs can be very high. Make sure you have enough money to cover necessities, two or three months of rent, meals, books, and insurance. With the informa-

U.S. Currency Denominations

Paper money (bills) and the presidents and famous people depicted on them:

$1 bill	George Washington
$5 bill	Abraham Lincoln
$10 bill	Alexander Hamilton
$20 bill	Andrew Jackson
$50 bill	Ulysses Grant

Coinage

a penny	1 cent (1/100th of a dollar)
a nickel	5 cents (5/100ths of a dollar)
a dime	10 cents (10/100ths of a dollar)
a quarter	25 cents (25/100ths of a dollar)

tion that you received from your school, decide on an initial budget before you leave for the United States. Allow a generous amount of money when doing so, and ask your parents or your sponsor for help.

Do not be confused between *minimum* and *average* costs. Determine the average expenses when you begin to establish your budget. Beyond the initial expenses listed above, your day-to-day budget should also include: clothing, entertainment, local transportation, taxes, and telephone charges. Some cities are more expensive than others.

HOUSING

Apart from your tuition, your housing costs will be your largest expense, so you should educate yourself on this topic. Begin by learning the terminology of American housing as it is explained below. See more on housing in chapter 9.

On-campus housing usually refers to residences located on your campus and run by your school. Most of the time, "on campus" housing offers you proximity to the library, computer equipment, the student center, recreation facilities, cafeterias, and your classes. However, sometimes school housing is not on campus and can be very expensive. It is very important to research all the details about your school's housing before you sign a contract. The housing office is the best place to offer such information. Contact it before you leave home.

Many schools also provide *off-campus* services, but you cannot use them until you arrive. These services can give you advice about locations, safety and security, and costs and utilities (such as telephone, gas, and electrical services). Ask to have information mailed to you about the differences in off-campus housing options.

Things to consider when you are researching possible housing options:
- *Co-ed or single-sex dorm*
- *Specialty dorm*
- *Fraternity (men) or sorority (women)*
- *On-campus dorm or off-campus apartment*

If you don't request on-campus housing, or if you plan to arrive in the United States before your dormitory is made available to you, you might be interested in temporary housing. Regular hotels can be expensive, but your international student advisor or housing office has information about affordable facilities located near your school.

Obtaining housing can be very difficult, but if you arrive early and do some research before you come to the United States, the process will be much easier. Be certain to include a housing search in your planning.

While you are preparing your original budget, remember that there is a general rule: Your monthly rent will approach 25 percent to 33 percent of your total monthly expenses. Rent costs are widely different throughout the United States. Consult your university catalog in the housing section. There should be information on the average cost of both on and off-campus housing. Once you have added housing to your monthly budget, don't forget to figure in that annual 5 percent increase in costs.

INSURANCE AND HEALTH CARE

All J-1 students and many F-1 students attending school in the United States are required to retain an insurance policy. In many programs, it is mandatory to enroll in your school's insurance program.

Insurance is very important for you because the United States does not have a national health program or social medical care. This means the cost of medical care and emergency health needs are not met by the federal, state, or city governments. All costs are paid by the individual. Medical care in the United States is very expensive, and your school hopes that you will never be affected by any serious type of medical situation.

However, if your school does have a mandatory plan, become acquainted with the specifics of the policy. Do not attempt to *waive*, or avoid, such coverage unless you retain a comparable policy. If your school does not have a mandatory program, do not ignore this issue because it appears to save money. Ask your international student advisor to show you brochures from various insurance companies offering plans specifically for international students and families.

When you review these plans, learn what the following terms mean and how they will affect your situation:

premium: the cost of coverage for a specified period of time

pre-existing condition: an illness you have been treated for prior to your current coverage

preventive care: annual medical care examination to maintain good health

deductible: the amount that you, the policy holder, are required to pay before your insurance coverage becomes effective

copayment: the amount you must pay on any claims you submit

If you obtain "J" visa status, you must hold an insurance policy that meets the following requirements:

- Major medical benefits must be at least $50,000
- Repatriation benefits must be at least $7,500
- Medical evacuation must be covered for at least $10,000
- The deductible for each accident or illness may not exceed $500
- Policy may not unreasonably exclude coverage for perils inherent to the activities of the exchange program

ARRIVAL IN THE UNITED STATES

On the airplane, you will be asked to begin completing your I-94. Make sure the name and date of birth you enter on the I-94 is the same as the one that appears on

Before You Leave for the United States, Have You. . . ?

❏ Made your flight reservation?

❏ Received details and an address from your school where to go upon your arrival? If you are not met by someone you know at the airport, find out how to get there from the airport, and how much you should expect to pay for that transportation.

❏ Prepared the recommended currency?

❏ Brought your passport and I-20 on the plane with you?

❏ Brought your admission letter and financial documentation?

❏ Packed your registration materials?

❏ Found out the general climate of the region you are visiting?

❏ Brought clothes that you will need during the immediate season?

❏ Brought electrical adapters for your appliances?

❏ Not packed too many bulky items such as blankets or pillows, since you can buy these later?

❏ Brought your prescribed medication, if any?

❏ Refilled your prescriptions for long-term use, if necessary?

❏ Brought an English translation of your medical history?

❏ Completed your school's immunization and vaccination require-ments and bring records with you?

❏ Brought with you the addresses and telephone numbers of your school, housing, bank, and American friends?

❏ Brought copies of your birth certificate, driver's license, and aca-demic transcripts?

your I-20 and in your passport. Have your passport, I-20, admission letter, and financial documentation available so you can present them upon entry to the United States.

If you hold more than one passport, use the one that corresponds to the country of citizenship on your I-20.

You can use an I-20 from one school in order to enter the United States even though you used another school's I-20 to obtain your F-1 visa. But you must report to the school which issued the I-20 you used to enter the United States.

If you forgot your I-20 or you packed it in your luggage by mistake, but you still have your passport with your F-1 visa stamp, request an I-515 form upon your inspection at the U.S. port. This document allows you to obtain F-1 status, gives you a month to obtain a new I-20 or locate your old one, and send it to the appropriate INS Office. If this happens, please notify your international student office at the earliest possible convenience.

Your luggage and your immigration documents will be inspected when you arrive. The INS Inspector will review your passport, visa, I-20 and I-94 (which is in three parts). They may also ask for your admission letter and financial documents. If everything is in order, the officer will stamp and staple one part of your I-94 and the bottom page of your I-20 ID copy. Your passport, I-20 ID, and I-94 are very, very important documents. Do not lose them.

The stamps indicate the port from which you entered the United States and on which date. The Inspector will write D/S on your I-94 and on your I-20 ID in the upper right corner. If he did not write D/S and did not issue an I-515, do not hesitate to ask why. This is usually an innocent oversight, but if it is not corrected at that time, it can be very difficult to do so at a later time.

The D/S notation means "duration of status." To figure out what "duration of status" means, you should go to section 5 on your I-20, where it states "complete studies not later than (date)." The date of your "duration of status" is that date plus 60 days. This 60 days is actually a "grace period" in which you must re-enroll, transfer to another school, apply for change or status (such as to a work visa), or leave the country. Failure to do so is to "fall out of status" and illegal.

If you are a J-1 student, look at section 3 on you IAP-66 where it states "from (date) to (date)," and add 30 days for "your duration of status" date.

Life in the University Community

Southwestern University

Life in the University Community | **8**

THE PEOPLE

When you attend a university, you do more than simply take classes: You become part of a complex community. Knowing who is who in that community will make your life a little easier. This chapter begins with a description of administrative staff who affect the direction and focus of your school, but whom you probably won't deal with directly. You'll then read about student services staff, faculty, and your fellow students, all of whom will have a considerable impact on your day-to-day experiences.

Administrative Staff

The administrative staff is the group of individuals who lead and manage the school at the most senior level.

- The **board of trustees** of the university is comprised of members of academia, industry, government, and the local community. The board is responsible for financial and policy matters related to the university.

- The **president** of the university is the chief administrator. Directly responsible to the board of trustees of the university, the president implements policy for the school.

- The **provost** is the chief academic officer. The provost is responsible for curriculum and technically in charge of faculty (though in reality, departments deal with their own faculty directly). This position reports to the president.

Student Services Staff

The student services staff interacts with students in order to ensure that the school is run smoothly.

- The *bursar* collects money for tuition and other student fees. Whenever you must pay a fee for something, such as a transcript, you will pay at the bursar's office, obtain a receipt, and present the receipt to the registrar.

- The *registrar* is responsible for students' academic records. You need to speak to the registrar if you have any scheduling problems or need copies of university-related student documents such as your transcript, schedule of classes, etcetera.

- The *ombudsman* is a person who receives complaints and helps mediate between students, faculty, and administration. If you have a complaint and feel that it not being fairly addressed by the responsible party, that complaint should be taken to the ombudsman's office.

- The *dean* heads a college within a university (such as the college of engineering). It is the dean's responsibility to enforce the university, college, and departmental policies set by various committees in the university. For this reason, most disciplinary actions are initiated from the dean's office. On the other hand, the dean is often the initiator of awards; for example, the dean's list.

- The *department head* or *chair* is responsible for the administrative functions of a specific department, such as the department of communications. The department chair is probably the person to whom you would go for any academic issues.

- The *foreign student advisor* is responsible for insuring that international students follow INS regulations and remain in compliance with their F-1 visas.

- The *academic advisor* helps students select their courses in order to fulfill various requirements. After selecting classes for the semester, you need to get your schedule approved by the academic advisor. During the first two years of study, your academic advisor will be a faculty member or from a special office of academic advising. Once you choose a major in your later years of study, you will be assigned a faculty advisor, a professor within your department.

- The *faculty advisor* directs your major course of study to insure that you have fulfilled the requirements of the major. Good faculty advisors will help you select the courses which are most relevant to your interests.

Faculty/Academic Staff

There are five types of faculty on a university campus. There is very little difference among these types of professors in a classroom setting, but their responsibilities outside of class may vary.

Tenured and *nontenured full-time professors* have an office on campus and will schedule office hours, a set time once or twice a week when students can privately discuss academic work. Professors will be assigned a number of students for academic advising.

Oftentimes, the name of an office is related to the topic of your questions. The residential life (or housing) office deals with housing; the registrar's office deals with registration; the admissions office deals with admission and enrollment; and the dean's office of your field of study answers academic questions.

Adjunct professors are instructors who work part time on a semester-to-semester basis. They may or may not have a private office and are thus less likely to be available outside of the classroom for extra help and do not engage in academic advising.

Campus Life: Whom to Contact

Bursar:	for financial questions
Registrar:	for course registration, to drop or add a course
Ombudsman:	for university-related matters of dispute
Academic Department Head:	to declare a major
Academic advisor:	for course and schedule approval
Professors:	for academic advisement and course-related questions
Secretaries:	for reported grades and transcripts

Visiting professors are instructors who have tenure at another university but are spending a semester or a year at another institution. Visiting professors will usually be assigned an office and will hold office hours, but they do not advise students at the host university.

Teaching assistants, or *TAs*, are graduate students who work alone or with a professor to teach a course. If your course has a TA and you need extra help with the subject matter, you should probably see this person first. TAs hold office hours but will not do academic advising.

Depending upon the university, the advisory system, and the student, the degree to which you will actually be advised will vary. In some universities, particularly larger schools, students are quite independent and are responsible for devising their own schedule with only perfunctory approval of the academic or faculty advisor. Other institutions will work much more intimately with students to prevent any problems or potential problems that could develop in a student's academic career.

Secretaries and *administrative assistants* handle the day-to-day administration of a department. They schedule professors' appointments, take care of correspondence, and perform clerical duties. If you need general information about the department, exam dates and times, or need to leave a message with your professor, these are the people you should contact.

Of course, the people that you will have the most contact with are other students. The American university system includes many types of students. Some students choose to go to university in their local areas, or they can move to another state to attend school. They can complete a degree in the standard four years, or they can attend part time and take many more years to earn a degree. Because of this flexibility, you will take classes with a diverse group of students.

Students

Resident Students: There are two types of resident student: Those who are originally from the local community, and those who have moved to the campus from another location. Approximately 80 percent of students attend university within their home state.

Commuter Students: Some schools, such as community colleges, are called *commuter colleges*. Most students who attend these schools live at home and attend school during the day—they may be students with full-time jobs, adults who are returning to school, or people hoping to refresh their professional skills. Universities that are located in large urban areas will often attract many commuter students.

Part-Time Students: Part time-students tend to be commuter students; that is, they live and work in the community while taking fewer than 12 credit hours per semester. Part-time students, because of work and family constraints, often attend night classes.

Returning Adult Students: These students are individuals who have waited several years after high school to attend college. Their university experience is often very different, as they are much older than the average student and may have other responsibilities such as a family or a job. However, the American university is open to all who want to study, and making the decision later in life to get a degree does not have to be a handicap. At the graduate level, it is not uncommon for students to be thirty or forty years of age while working toward an M.A. or Ph.D.

UNIVERSITY-TOWN RELATIONSHIP

The relationship between the town and the university will vary greatly from school to school. Any *college town* (a town where the university itself is the major industry) will have an economy that is highly dependent upon the university population for income. Typical college-dependent businesses include: bookstores, cafés, sandwich shops, bars, vintage clothing stores, and record stores. Depending upon the university you attend, there may be a very good relationship between the university and the town, or there may be a great deal of tension. Local governments sometimes enact laws that are clearly directed to control the student population, such as ordinances regarding parking or noise levels. Universities that are located in big cities, such as New York, Chicago, and Los Angeles, tend not to have too many conflicts with the surrounding community as these schools are more likely to blend in with the larger economy. Usually, the greatest tension in bigger cities regards real estate and zoning laws rather than specific student-related issues.

EXTRACURRICULAR ACTIVITIES

Every university offers a wide range of activities outside of the classroom. Some activities will be specific to your university, others will be divisions of national or international organizations. Following is a sample list:

Area Studies: Undergraduate Society for Neuroscience; Women in Communications; Spanish Club; American Library Association Student Chapter; American Society of Civil Engineers; School Newspaper

Hobbies: Chess Club; Yoga Society; Hiking Club; Photography Club

Political and Social Causes: Gay and Lesbian Student Organization; Young Democrats; Young Republicans; Korean Student Association; Student Senate

Sports: Soccer; Hockey; Tennis; Basketball

Religious Groups: Christian Student Association; Islamic Student Organization

Activities and clubs are very important to American students, not only because they are opportunities for engaging in an enjoyable pastime, but because employers like applicants to be well-rounded. Check your university's website for a description of the student organizations.

COMPLETING THE DEGREE

Credits

The amount of work one does at a university is measured in *credits*. Although each university has its own formula for dividing up the academic year, students in a typical undergraduate program take 12–18 credit hours per semester (an average of 15 credits per semester), two semesters per year. This means that the student is required to be in class a total of 15 hours per week. Most classes are worth 3 credits each, though some courses, such as physical education, may carry fewer credits while others, such as remedial skills courses, carry no credits. Most degrees require that a student earn a total of 120 credits. The 15 hours per week can be deceiving, since this is only the time that you spend in lectures. Be prepared to spend at least one to one-and-a-half hours studying and doing research for each hour that you spend in the classroom (this is why your I-20 will be valid in a full-time program).

GPA

As we mentioned in chapter 5, our progress through the degree program is measured by your *GPA (Grade Point Average)*. Each school has its own method of awarding grades, but most universities use a four-point scale, with 4.0 the best, and 1.0 the worst. Anything below 1.0 is considered Failing.

Some schools will offer intermediate grades, such as an AB or B+.

Grade

Your grade for an individual course is based on a few factors. Most courses will have two or three exams as well as quizzes, a research paper, lab work, oral presentations, and class participation. Undergraduate students are not tested with a comprehensive exam at the end of the course, as they are in many other countries. Instead, students are tested throughout the semester. It is not unusual for an American student to be preparing for a test every week. Graduate programs may base the grade strictly on research, writing, lab work, and/or class participation. In graduate courses, students might only take one exam at the end of the course of study.

American students are obsessed with their GPAs, and for a good reason. If your GPA falls below 2.0 (the equivalent of a C), you may be put on academic probation. At the graduate level, probation generally occurs if your grade falls below 3.0 (or a B). In such a situation, you have one semester to raise your grade or you will be expelled from school. Unfortunately, many international students are not prepared for this system of ongoing testing and evaluation, and approximately 30 percent are expelled within the first year.

Tests

Professors generally use three types of exam: quizzes, midterms, and final exams. The amount of weight that an individual exam has in determining your final grade is determined by the instructor. Most professors distribute a syllabus at the beginning of the semester which outlines the course requirements, including the grading procedure. If you are not sure about how your grade is being determined, feel free to ask the professor.

Issues of Harrassment

Most universities have clearly defined guidelines for **harassment**—whether sexual, racial, or religious. Punishment for harassment can range from an admonishment to expulsion. If information regarding harassment is not included during your orientation, you will want to find out about these policies. If you feel that you are being harassed due to sexual, racial, or religious difference, report it immediately. There is no need to remain silent if harassment is interfering with your studies or peace of mind.

Quizzes are short exams given frequently throughout the course. Individually, they are worth less of your course grade than midterms or finals, but together, they can add up to be worth half of your overall grade.

Midterms and *finals* test your comprehensive knowledge of the subject over the course of the semester. As the name implies, midterms are administered approximately midway through the semester. Finals are given at the end of the semester.

Types of Test Question

Multiple-choice questions are very popular in American classes, particularly in classes with a large number of students. The typical multiple-choice question offers four or five answer choices from which to choose.

American students are pretty familiar with this type of question by the time they attend college. If you have never taken an exam with multiple-choice questions— choose the best answer. If you do not know the answer, try to eliminate one or two answers that you know are wrong and then guess. Here is an example.

1. The *Declaration of Independence* was signed in:
    A. New York City on August 8, 1770.
    B. Dallas, Texas on February 14, 1786.
    C. Philadelphia on July 4, 1776.
    D. Boston on May 5, 1775.

True or false questions take the form of a statement. You must determine whether the statement is true or false. Typically, the letters T and F are used to indicate your answer. Here is an example.

_____ George Washington is called "the father of our country" because he
had 37 children.

Short-answer questions provide a small space where you can write in your answer. Information such as names, dates, and vocabulary words is tested with this type of question. Here is an example.

We hold these truths to be self-evident that all men are created
_____ and that they are endowed by their creator with certain
inalienable rights, among these are life, liberty and the pursuit of _____.

Essay questions are more subjective than objective. These usually require longer answers written in narrative form. You may be asked to describe an event, compare two theories, or critique a reading. Many universities use *blue books*: small, official notebooks in which you write your essay answers.

Categories of Courses

As we have discussed in chapter 3, you will be taking two types of courses: those for distribution requirements (general education), and those for your major. Work closely with your academic advisor to determine which distribution classes will be most satisfying for you.

Distribution requirements

In the early years of university study, students must choose from various areas of human knowledge including the humanities, sciences, communication, and often, foreign language. Each university has its own program, but all major universities have this requirement. Undergraduates are not required to declare a major until the end of the second or beginning of the third year. One advantage of this is that you are not locked into a field of study when you first begin school. Many students enter the university with a particular major in mind, but, after taking distribution courses, discover that they have an interest or talent in an area they never considered before.

You'll probably hear some students complain about having to take distribution courses: "I'm never going to conduct a symphony, so why do I have to take music appreciation?" Try to look at this requirement as an opportunity to learn something new and exciting. Most universities offer enough choices that you can easily find something interesting. The University of Wisconsin, for example, allows humanities students to fulfill a science requirement with the course "Physics for Poets."

Most colleges require at least the humanities students to take a foreign language. Check with your academic adviser: Some schools will exempt you from this requirement if your native language is not English. All students have to take at

While tests are usually graded on a scale of 1 to 100, instructors may "grade on a curve" according to how the entire class performs. Let's say that on a test, the highest grade is 70% of the answers correct, and the lowest grade is 20% of the answers correct. The majority of people scored in the 40–60% range. So the 70% grade, which would normally be recorded as a C, is recorded as an A, and the rest of the grades are adjusted accordingly.

least one writing course, which you will be placed into after a writing test. Many schools require students to take physical education classes as well.

Graduate programs are more highly specialized, and grad students may not be required to take a course outside of the major area of study.

Major courses

Once you have declared a major field of study, you will have to take certain *required courses*; all students who receive a degree in that major have to take those courses.

Some courses will require you to work on projects in groups. And if you have a laboratory section within a science course, you'll work with a "lab partner."

For example, history majors would be required to take six credits (two courses) of European history. They can choose from among courses like Postwar German History, French Intellectual History, The Italian Renaissance, and Medieval English History.

Types of Classes

The actual classroom experience can be arranged in a number of different ways:

Large lecture with discussion or lab section is typically an introductory or lower-level class. At large universities, classes may be held in an auditorium with 1,000 students in attendance. The professor speaks for most of the lecture, and if there is a discussion period, it is brief. Students also meet in much smaller groups, called sections, which are typically led by graduate students and/or teaching assistants. During the discussion or lab section, you will be able to ask questions and engage in more thorough discussion. If the course is in science or engineering, you may use this time to conduct laboratory experiments.

Certain courses, particularly the higher-level courses, will have prerequisites. A prerequisite is a course that you must take before being admitted to a more advanced course. For example, Calculus 101 is a prerequisite for Calculus 201.

Medium-sized class has about 20–60 students. Most of the time is spent on teacher instruction, but there is more freedom to ask questions and have discussion than in a large lecture class.

Seminar usually has a small number of students. The purpose of the class is discussion, and the instructor functions mainly to direct the conversation.

Daily Life

- If you're a full-time undergraduate student, you'll spend about three hours a day in class. You may not have class on Tuesday and Thursday until 2:00 P.M., and your last class may end by 11:00 A.M. on Monday, Wednesday, and Friday.

- Class is often optional. Very few professors take attendance. Many won't bother to collect homework or check to see if you've done the assigned reading. If you don't show up for class, keep up with the reading, or complete the homework, you performance will suffer on exam day.

- The distractions are nonstop—from parties to concerts and student programs. You'll have to find a good balance between your studies and your entertainment, and it will take a lot of self-discipline.

- Final exams are intense. Nothing you have done in life will prepare you for finals: minimal sleep, maximum pressure. Up to 40 percent of your grade for the entire term is determined in a one-week period.

[Adapted from *Making it Count*, by Patrick S. O'Brien/*Newsweek* article]

Choosing a Major

At some time during your second year of undergraduate study, you will be asked to declare a major. Your *major* is the field of study that you will focus on for the remainder of your education. Some schools have very open policies, allowing any student who maintains the minimum GPA to enter the major. Others may have stricter admission policies.

Many students will also choose a *minor*, that is, an area of specialization like the major but one in which you take fewer courses. Students usually choose a minor to complement the major, or to add another dimension to their major area of study. For example, a business major

Occasionally, a course will require an audition, meaning the submission of a portfolio or a writing sample. The instructor then decides if you are qualified to take the class.

Cultural Adaptation

While there is no way to predict how quickly you will adapt to the American culture, you should realize that you are not the only person to experience a range of feelings. First, you will probably be very excited at the prospect of a new experience, but you may also feel a little regret and stress at the thought of leaving family and friends.

• Keep in touch with people from your home country. There's a good chance there are a few other students from your country at your university; there may even be an established international student organization. Interact and get advice from people who have been in America longer than you. If they survived, so can you.

• If you are feeling very depressed, see a counselor at the university health center. University psychologists are especially trained to assist with the stress-related problems that students typically experience. There may even be a counselor who specializes in helping foreign students who are undergoing culture shock. Americans are generally accepting of mental health counseling and you should not feel embarrassed to see someone.

• Exercise. This may seem like a strange tip, but staying in good physical condition does wonders for your mental health. It is a great way to get rid of stress and feelings of frustration and sadness. Most universities have good athletic facilities that are free or inexpensive to students. Take advantage of them.

• Try to remember that this is a normal phase in adjusting to a new culture. It will pass and you will feel better eventually.

• Keep in mind that you are not the only one in a new environment. All of the freshmen, transfer students or new graduate students must also adjust to new environment. For many freshmen, this is likely their first time away from home, even if it's within the United States. Some freshmen students react with mild "homesickness," while others with more severe reactions may turn to substance abuse.

might minor in Russian. Upon graduating, he would have an advantage in obtaining a job with a company that does business in Eastern Europe.

Some universities will allow students with exceptional ability and ambition to carry a *double major.* These students meet the requirements of two completely independent courses of study.

If, at some point after declaring your major and taking courses within it, you decide that it really is not the field for you, you can *change your major.* Depending upon how far you have advanced in your original major, this may affect how long it will take you to get your degree. If you have just started your major, you may be able to finish in four years. However, if you decide to switch when you are one semester away from graduating, you may have to revise your plans and study for an additional period.

EMPLOYMENT OPPORTUNITIES

If you have a valid F-1 visa, you may work *on campus* without prior approval from the Immigration and Naturalization Service (INS). You must be enrolled full time, and you are limited to 20 hours per week of employment. It is unlawful for the university to fire or lay off an American employee in order to hire a foreign worker. Many schools require that you obtain authorization from your FSA (Foreign Student Advisor), but it is unnecessary to contact the INS for permission.

If you are a graduate student, on-campus employment can also mean employment by companies located off-campus that have a research contract or educational affiliation with your university.

To qualify for work *off-campus*, you must meet the following conditions:
1. You must be in good academic standing and enrolled in full-time study.
2. You must have completed one academic year of study.
3. You must have a letter of recommendation from the foreign student adviser.
4. You must demonstrate severe economic hardship due to one of the following reasons. Economic hardship is not defined by poor planning on the student's part or by normal increases in the cost of living.
   - Loss of financial aid or on-campus employment through no fault of the student
   - Major currency fluctuations

- Inordinate tuition or living expense increases
- Unexpected financial changes in the students' source of support
- Unexpected expenses
- On-campus employment opportunities are unavailable

To secure work authorization you must submit Form I-538 to your FSA for certification. You then must submit the certified I-538, Form I-20 (your student copy), Form I-765 with filing fee, and evidence that supports your claim of economic hardship to your local INS office. Upon approval, you will receive a one-year employment authorization card which allows you to work up to 20 hours per week.

Practical Training Opportunities

Practical training is an integral part of many American students' education. Recognizing this, the INS has divided practical training into two categories, curricular and optional. In order to qualify for practical training authorization you must have been a full-time F-1 student for at least nine consecutive months.

Curricular practical training includes work that is either required by a work/study program, earns you course credit, or is mandatory for graduation. In any case, a faculty member must oversee the course. You obtain authorization for curricular practical training through your FSA. While there is no time limit on curricular practical training, if you have worked more than one year in curricular practical training, you would be ineligible for optional practical training.

Optional practical training must be directly related to your major field of study and can be granted for a total of 12 months maximum (this means you can work three months a year for four years, or work two periods of six months, or any other combination that results in a total of one year or less). Optional practical training may occur during or after completion of your studies and requires authorization from the INS. You must get your FSA to endorse Form I-538. Then you will apply directly to your local INS office for an employment authorization document (EAD) by filing Form I-765 with fee and endorsed Form I-538. Your FSA can provide further details regarding optional practical training.

The Essentials of Living in the United States

Tufts University

The Essentials of Living in the United States

HOUSING

In preparing for your study-abroad experience in the United States, one of your first priorities will be to find a comfortable, safe, and affordable place in which to live.

Your school will provide you with information concerning housing options both *on* and *off campus*. Review this information carefully to help you decide what type of accommodations are right for you and your budget.

On-Campus Housing

Most schools have on-campus housing, referred to as *residence halls* or *dormitories* (*dorms*, for short). On-campus housing is located directly on the grounds of the school. Most universities require incoming students to live on campus for the first year. Many new students find living on campus to be easier than living off campus, since there are fewer responsibilities. On-campus accommodations must be reserved far in advance of the start of the academic year, so be sure to communicate with the admissions office of your chosen school.

For most students, dorm life is an important part of the university experience. It is a great way to make new friends, and being close to campus activities and resources is very appealing. In addition, the residence hall staff is available 24 hours a day to assist students, making campus housing a comfortable, secure living environment.

Dormitories can vary a great deal, ranging from the traditional-style dorms to more modern apartments. Students are almost always required to share a room with one other student (a *roommate*). While some single rooms are available, they are in high demand and unlikely to be given to a new freshman.

Living on campus, however, is not without its problems. Dorm life can be noisy, distracting, and crowded. Some people find dorm food a bit institutional. And, finally, some campuses close their dormitories over major holidays (such as Christmas and Thanksgiving), temporarily displacing students from their rooms.

Some dorms are arranged so that rooms are lined up along hallways. Others may be arranged into *suites*, which have a group of bedrooms and a common room. Dormitories can be single-sex or coed (both sexes living in the same building), though you will always have a roommate the same sex as you.

Dorm rooms provide students with very minimal furnishings—a bed, desk, dresser, and closet. Bathroom facilities are generally shared among residents of the same sex. Many dorms also have lounge and television areas, computer rooms, and study areas. Because accommodations are extremely basic, most students take the time to decorate their space, creating a comfortable, homelike environment.

- *It might cost you up to $200 to install a telephone.*
- *Most people have telephone answering machines.*
- *Long-distance and international phone calls are expensive. Shop around for a telephone service with discounted rates or pick up a few discount long-distance calling cards.*
- *Many schools provide students with email (electronic mail via a computer) accounts.*
- *If you live on-campus, you'll be given a post office mailbox.*

Dormitories are run by *resident assistants*, or *RAs*, who are usually upper-level students trained to help you with problems related to living in the dorms. RAs also help to enforce university policies regarding the dorm, such as prohibitions against excessive noise or alcohol. If you have a personal problem that you would like to discuss, or need advice regarding campus life, the RA is often a good person to speak to.

Having a roommate in a dorm is a new experience for everyone. While most universities will try to match you with an appropriate roommate by asking you about your personal habits (whether you smoke, for example), and your intended major, adjusting to the experience of living with another person in such small quarters is quite an adjustment. Because most American universities strive for diversity, as an international student, you will likely be paired with an American.

Your dorm roommate will probably be the first person that you get to know at your new school, and this person may become your closest friend or your biggest irritation. Differences in individual living styles and personalities can lead to conflicts between roommates. While most students try to work out their differences, some students find it too difficult to do that and so request a change for the remainder of the term. If you and your roommate are not able to get along, speak to your RA.

134

If you share any of the concerns listed above, off-campus housing may provide an exciting alternative to on-campus living.

Off-Campus Housing

Many students choose to move off campus to a nearby house or apartment as they progress in their studies. Even then, most students find it necessary to live with a roommate (though this does not usually mean sharing a bedroom). If you are a graduate student, you may have the opportunity to live on campus but, more often than not, you will live in an apartment off campus. Check the university housing office for apartment availability as well as notice boards to see who is looking for a roommate.

Living with strangers is not unusual at U.S. schools. If you decide to share an apartment off campus, try to speak with all of the people that you will be living with. Do they have any pets (animals)? Do they have a lot of parties? Do they smoke? This last point can be a very important issue for a potential roommate.

Most schools have off-campus housing offices to assist students with their housing needs. You'll also find listings of available apartments and of people seeking roommates. Keep your eyes open around campus, too, as additional listings are often posted on bulletin boards and in the local and school newspapers. Remember, finding comfortable, safe, and affordable housing takes time and effort. Be sure to start your housing search well in advance of the start of the academic year.

To offset the high cost of housing, many students seek roommates with whom to share their apartments. Take the time to identify what you want in terms of the cost, size, security, and location of the apartment. Don't forget to ask about availability of laundry and exercise facilities, and supermarkets.

Americans have very strong opinions about the issue of smoking. Be sure to be open and honest with any potential roommates, or you might end up with a big problem.

Renting an apartment in the United States requires signing a written contract (a *lease*), which outlines the terms of the rental agreement. A lease is a binding legal document that specifies the monthly rental price, the number of tenants, and the length of time you may reside in the apartment. Most leases are for one or two years.

Before you sign a lease, read it carefully to be sure you understand and accept the terms of the rental agreement. You should be aware that landlords require a securi-

Discovering American Values Through Proverbs

Proverb	Value
Cleanliness is next to godliness.	Cleanliness
A penny saved is a penny earned.	Thrift
Waste not, want not.	Frugality
Early to bed, early to rise, makes a man healthy, wealthy, and wise.	Discipline
God helps those who help themselves.	Initiative
It's not whether you win or lose; it's how you play the game.	Good sportsmanship
A man's home is his castle.	Private property
You've made your own bed, now lie in it.	Responsibility

ty deposit of up to one month's rent upon signing the lease. A security deposit is "safety money" for the landlord in case you damage the apartment or abandon the property abruptly. Security deposits are returned to you at the end of your tenancy, as long as the apartment is in good condition and the rent is paid in full.

Failing to respect the terms of the lease can result in eviction. In addition to following the provisions of the lease, maintaining a good relationship with the landlord and other tenants is important for a comfortable living environment.

Living off campus is a big responsibility. A few apartments are furnished, but the majority are not. For those, you would have to purchase all your basic housewares and furnishings. Many students purchase these items secondhand (used) to save money. Off-campus living also requires arranging and paying for basic utilities (water, gas, and electricity), local and long-distance telephone service, cable television service, and other amenities. Home security (door and window locks, smoke

---

Reading a Newspaper Ad for an Apartment

A "classified ad" is a small newspaper advertisement or listing that "offers" an apartment or room. Because of the shortage of space, these ads include many word abbreviations. Try to figure out what the sample ad below means:

Larkspur Listings

Lg 2 bdrm apt. w/ hi ceils on Creek Lane nr downtown avail 9/1; 3rd fl, lg lvrm & decor fpl; sep sleeping loft 10x12 over kitchen makes this apt excel for shares; 3 clsts; lndry in bldg, g/e incl: $1,750/mo; Refs req'd; no fee. Owner 621-3532.

Translation:

Large 2 bedroom apartment with high ceilings on Creek Lane near downtown. Available September 1. Located on third floor, large living-room and decorative fireplace. Separate sleeping loft 10x12 feet over the kitchen makes this apartment excellent for shares (roommates). 3 closets; laundry in the building, gas and electric (utilities) are included in price. Cost: $1,750 per month. Personal references required. No additional fee. Call the owner at 621-3532.

---

detectors) is also a renter's responsibility. Renters are entitled to a well-kept building that is clean and livable. General maintenance and repair is the responsibility of the landlord. If a landlord is not maintaining a well-kept building and your apartment is in disrepair, notify the local housing department to report the situation.

In spite of the number of responsibilities associated with off campus living, many students enjoy the increased privacy and greater independence. Like most situations, living off campus has a few less desirable features. For some, living off campus can be an isolating, lonely experience. It also requires a reliable means of transportation (car, bus, or subway) and, in some cases, a significant amount of commuting time. Finally, signing a lease typically "locks" a renter into a one- to two-year housing commitment. Breaking a lease can result in losing your security deposit.

Whether you live on or off campus, it is important to have comfortable, safe accommodations during your stay in the United States. Use this checklist to help you find the right spot.

Apartment Hunting Checklist

❏ Who will you be sharing the apartment with?

❏ Will you have your own bedroom?

❏ Is the cost of the apartment acceptable to you?
  • Rent
  • Security deposit (often the equivalent of one month's rent)
  • First month *and* last month's rent required upon signing the lease

❏ Is the location of the apartment convenient?
  • To public transportation and/or to car parking
  • To and from school
  • To shopping

❏ Is the apartment safe?
  • During the daytime and after dark
  • Is it on the ground floor (street level)?
  • Are there good locks on the doors (and windows if necessary)?

❏ Will you be required to install and pay for utilities separately?
  • Heat and electricity
  • Water
  • Gas (if necessary)
  • Telephone and television

❏ Does the apartment contain any of the following items?
  • Furniture
  • Dishes and kitchen utensils
  • Bed linens and towels
  • Electrical appliances

The Greek System

One option available to undergraduates is the *fraternity/sorority system,* often referred to as the Greek system because the names of the fraternities and sororities are composed of two or three Greek letters. A fraternity is a social organization made up of male students who live together in a large house. A sorority is the equivalent organization for women.

While many Greek organizations are involved in some form of community service, their primary function is social. At the beginning of the school year, fraternities and sororities recruit new members who, after being chosen, are inducted into the fraternity of sorority house.

FOOD

At first glance, this may not seem like a topic that needs much explanation. Fast food from McDonald's and Burger King can be found in almost every country in the world. However, every region of the United States has a reputation for its own local specialties, such as Tex-Mex, Cajun, and southern barbecue.

Americans usually eat three meals a day: breakfast, lunch, and dinner. *Breakfast* may include cereal, eggs and meat (bacon, ham, or sausage), and bread. Breakfast is very popular among most Americans, and some restaurants serve breakfast foods all day long. *Lunch,* eaten around 1:00 P.M., is usually a sandwich and potato chips, or soup and a salad.

Dinner, the largest meal of the day, is served between 5:30 P.M. and 9 P.M. and is usually based around a hot meat dish with side portions of vegetables and potatoes. Dinner is perceived as a social occasion and is therefore the longest meal of the day.

- *Every region of the United States has a reputation for local specialties.*
- *Dinner is the longest meal of the day.*
- *The typical portion size in a restaurant will seem ridiculously large.*
- *It is not uncommon for students to gain 5–10 pounds in their first year in the United States.*

Healthy Eating in the United States

It takes some thought and discipline to eat a healthy diet in this country. There is a tendency to overeat here, and the typical restaurant portion size can seem unnecessarily large. Stores and cafeterias serve many packaged and processed foods that contain a lot of sugar, salt, and preservatives. In fact, many international students experience weight gains of 5–10 pounds during their first year in the United States. Takeout and delivery restaurants are usually located near schools: They will prepare meals for you to take home or have delivered to your residence. American college students often stay up late studying and eating snack food. If you are concerned about weight gain and general nutrition, try to not overeat. By the way, all packaged food is required by U.S. law to list the ingredients as well as the nutritional content. When you shop for your own food, read these nutrition labels.

Meal Plans

If you choose to live on campus, you will be asked to choose a cafeteria meal plan. A *meal plan* is a prepaid plan that provides meals in campus cafeterias. A complete meal plan covers breakfast, lunch, and dinner; while a partial meal plan covers one or two meals per day. Cafeterias typically offer a selection of hot meals, a salad bar, sandwiches, and vegetarian options.

Some Quotes about American Food

"The first thing my mother said to me when she saw me at the airport was, 'You're so fat!'"
—A student from Greece

"I tried to adapt to the times and types of meals in the U.S., and the result was quite disastrous. I found that it was much better to keep my eating habits. The major difference was having my main meal of three courses at lunch time and a light supper at night."
—An international student

"All of the breads can be really confusing."
—A student from Japan

It might also be possible to choose a meal plan if you live off campus. Though many off-campus students prefer to cook their own meals at home, you might want to eat one or two meals on campus while you are attending classes. Ask your admissions office about meal plan options for off-campus housing.

Some students living on campus choose not to purchase meal plans. There are advantages and disadvantages to this. School dining areas are great meeting places, and a meal plan can be very convenient. There can be problems, however: Food is served at specific times, the assortment of food may be limited, and the cost of the meal plan can be high. Cooking on your own is usually less expensive and gives you more freedom with the food you eat. Some school residence halls have kitchens that are shared by people on one floor or in a suite. If this is the case where you live, it is important to set some rules about the use of shared food and cooking utensils. It is also important to be open-minded about other people's eating habits.

Although Americans may have some strange preferences—diet sodas, fat-free foods, artificially flavored and sweetened desserts—homemade, farm grown and organic foods have become more popular in recent years. With a little effort, your culinary studies can be a fascinating adventure.

Staying Healthy

In preparing for your study experience in the United States, it is natural to be concerned about your overall health and well being. Staying healthy, both mentally and physically, is key to succeeding in your studies. Besides, getting sick is never a fun experience, especially when you are far from home. It is important for you to know that you have access to good health care while in the United States.

Maintaining a healthy lifestyle, a balanced diet, regular exercise, and plenty of rest will help you stay well. Try to keep a regular routine when it comes to eating, exercise, sports, and sleeping. Your diet in the United States will probably be different from what your body is used to. You may want to bring a good multivitamin to supplement your diet during your stay. And as some regions of the country experience severe hot and cold temperatures, dress appropriately for the climate in which you will be living.

HEALTH CARE

The United States health care system is among the best in the world, but it is extremely expensive. As an international students, you should know that the United States does not have a free or nationalized system of health care. In order to afford the high cost of medical care, most residents participate in a health insurance plan. For international students and their accompanying dependents, it is very important to have adequate health insurance coverage.

Most schools have health insurance plans for their students. If your school does not offer one, contact the international student office for the names of reputable insurance providers.

Many schools have health clinics on campus that provide a comprehensive range of medical services at reduced rates. It is a good idea to visit the health clinic when you arrive to familiarize yourself with its services.

If you have a serious medical emergency such as a broken bone or serious bleeding, do not hesitate to go to a hospital emergency room. If you are unable to get to the emergency room on your own, dial 911 on the telephone and an ambulance service will assist you immediately. Although off-campus health clinics and private doctors' offices are expensive, hospital emergency rooms are even more so. Hospital emergency room services should be used in urgent medical situations only.

Seeing a Doctor

Doctor-patient relationships differ from culture to culture. You may find that doctors in the United States provide patient care and treatment differently from what you are used to in your home county. For some international students, health care services here are intimidating. Knowing what to expect on a doctor's visit alleviates the fear and facilitates a more comfortable experience.

Health centers typically have various medical professionals providing patient care. Depending on your condition, you may be seen by a nurse, nurse practitioner, physician, physician's assistant, midwife, or specialist. All of these individuals are qualified medical professionals. Many health centers have a multilingual staff, so if you feel unable to express yourself clearly in English, request a translator.

Doctors in the United States typically see many patients in one day. Therefore, the amount of time they have with each person is limited. It's a good idea to write down a list of things you would like to discuss with the doctor and bring it to the appointment. Also, bring any medication you are taking, even if it was prescribed in your home country. This is important information for the doctor to know.

In the examining room, the doctor will ask a series of questions. Stay calm and answer the questions to the best of your knowledge. Remember, it is important for you to ask questions too. Always have the doctor clarify anything you are unclear about.

If you are uncomfortable with a doctor or a prescribed treatment, you have the right to get a *"second opinion"* from another medical professional. With more serious health problems, this is commonly done in the United States. Do not hesitate to seek out another professional's advice—doctors will not be insulted.

Here's what you should know before you visit a health clinic or doctor:

1. The hours of the health center
2. The appointment procedures
3. The payment policy (and what "insurance plans" are accepted by the clinic)
4. The wellness programs offered: nutritional counseling, birth control counseling, sexually transmitted disease prevention, psychological counseling, and stress management
5. The number of health care providers versus the number of patients

PLAYING IT SAFE

For most international students coming to the United States, safety is a big concern. Playing it safe at home, on campus, and in the community requires a few basic precautions.

Safety at Home

Whether you live on or off campus, creating a safe, comfortable living environment is important for your peace of mind and overall well being. A safe living environment starts with a few features such as:

1. **A solid door lock, and window locks if necessary.**

   If your apartment is on the ground floor (street level) or top floor, or if it has a fire escape, window locks are essential.

2. **A peep hole in the front door.**

   A peep hole allows you to see ("peep") who is on the opposite side of the door.

   Always look through it and ask visitors to identify themselves before opening the door.

3. **A smoke detector.**

   This is an alarm that automatically sounds off in the presence of smoke or fire. If there is a fire in the building while you are asleep, the smoke detector will awaken you.

As an additional precaution, list only your last name and first initial on mailboxes, doorbells, and in the telephone book. If you have questions about the security features of your residence, ask your superintendent or housing office for assistance.

In the United States, telemarketing calls (companies selling products or services over the telephone) to private homes are common. Some telemarketing calls are legitimate, while others are not. Be careful when taking calls from telemarketing representatives. Do not disclose personal information such as your address, bank account number, or credit card number to strangers over the telephone. Personal information is your private business and should not be shared with strangers.

Safety on Campus

Staying safe when you are out and about in the United States requires what can be called *"street smarts."* The following safety tips are examples of "street smarts" behaviors.

1. Never leave your personal belongings unattended in places such as classrooms, libraries, or restrooms—they might get stolen.
2. Avoid campus facilities (public restrooms, library stacks, and walking paths) late at night and early in the morning, when they are isolated. Many schools have an on-campus security service available to escort students home at night, so feel free to use it.
3. Walk in groups of two or more at night. Remember, there's safety in numbers!
4. Travel on busy, well-lighted streets with shops and pedestrian traffic. Avoid dark, deserted side streets and areas.
5. Don't visit parks at night.
6. Do not count your money in public. Keep your money concealed. Also, don't carry large sums of cash.
7. Don't let strangers trick you into giving them money. The tricks of con artists can appear dangerously innocent.

There are a few other issues you should be aware of. First, sexual harassment has become a serious and controversial issue for academic institutions across the United States. Sexual harassment affects men, women, faculty, and students alike. If you feel you have been a victim of sexual harassment, report the incident to your international student advisor, ombudsman, and campus authorities.

Second, be aware that illegitimate student clubs may exist on your college campus. While the far majority of clubs are legitimate student organizations, *cults* are typically religious or political groups interested in recruiting young new members for inappropriate reasons. Cults disrupt lives and harm people by forcing them to cut ties with their family and friends and to contribute a lot of money. Before joining a club, be sure it is recognized as a legitimate student organization.

BANKING

One of the first things you must do after arriving in the United States is to open a bank account. It is advisable to bring traveler's checks with you initially so that you won't have to carry around a lot of cash or store large sums of money in your residence. When looking for a bank, you will want to compare price, proximity to school and home, and the availability of automated teller machines (ATMs) in the community. Many banks want to attract the business of students and will offer special rates and discounts.

Banks typically charge **monthly fees** for bank usage. You might be charged for every check that you write, or for every cash withdrawal you make from an ATM. Even though these fees are individually small sums, they can add up quickly. Try to look for accounts that require as few monthly fees as possible. You'll need to fill out an application form and provide the necessary identification.

Types of Accounts

There are two types of bank accounts: savings and checking. A *savings* account earns interest on all money deposited; monthly statements are sent to show the accumulated interest. If you bring a lot of money to the United States (consult home banking institution in advance regarding the transfer of money overseas), you will want to open a savings account to keep the majority of funds. However, you will also need a checking account for daily, weekly, or monthly expenses.

A *checking* account usually does not earn interest on deposited funds but it does permit you to write checks for payment. The vast majority of people in the U.S. pay for most bills such as rent, telephone, and credit cards with checks. Another important point: People do not send cash in the mail in the United States.

Banking Tips

- *Banks charge a large fee for bounced checks (returned due to insufficient funds). If you write a check as payment, make sure your account has the money to cover it.*
- *People do not customarily send cash in the mail.*
- *Checks are the preferred payment for most bills, such as electric bills or credit card bills.*

After opening a checking account, you will receive a supply of blank checks and a checkbook for keeping track of all deposits and withdrawals. It is very important to keep track of all financial transactions! That way, you will have a paper record of your personal finances. At the end of each month, the bank will send you a statement listing all transactions it has recorded. Compare the statement with your personal record, deducting any extra fees and service charges. If there is a discrepancy, the bank can help you resolve it.

Your bank will give you an automated teller machine (*ATM*) card with a ***personal identification number*** (PIN). This card allows you to withdraw, deposit, or transfer money at automated banking machines in the community. Simply insert the ATM card and follow the instructions that appear on screen. Many ATMs in urban areas are now offering services in different languages. If possible, use ATMs in banks that have security guards and avoid using ATMs alone at night.

Student Quotes about Banking

"I think that it's hard for many students to understand the importance of knowing that you are going to be paying your own bills."
—*A student from Ecuador*

"Some banks have a hard time understanding that we have no social security number. If showing your IAP-66 doesn't help, consult your international advisor."
—*A student from Germany*

Credit Cards

After opening your bank account, you may receive applications for credit cards. If you need a credit card, you will have to submit an application, meet income and credit qualifications, and pay an annual fee. If you already have a credit card from your country, find out before you leave home whether it will be accepted in the United States and if there are extra service fees to use it here. Visa™, American Express™, and MasterCard™ are the most widely accepted cards in the United States. There are other cards, such as the Discover™ card, but they are not as widely used. Credit cards are also offered by stores and gas companies. If using such cards, it is critical that you pay your monthly credit card bills promptly: Interest rates on late payments are extremely high, and many people find themselves paying enormous late fees. Be careful about charging more than you can afford.

TRAVEL

One important aspect of studying abroad is to experience another culture. While you are studying in America, try to acquire a deeper understanding of daily life, practices, and values. Get to know your campus, but also the wider community. The United States is a fantastically diverse country that invites travel almost everywhere.

There are many inexpensive ways to see the United States. Start by purchasing a travel book, researching on the Internet, calling a visitors' bureau, and reading the travel sections in newspapers. Many newspapers advertise travel packages as well as discounted airfares. Many students use the bus as a less-expensive form of transportation. Trains offer a more comfortable way to travel, but can be more expensive than buses. Other students rent cars (you must be 25 years of age and have a credit card in your name) and travel in small groups.

An easy way to meet other students while you travel is to enroll in the group trips offered by schools or student clubs. Some parts of the country have organizations such as the YMCA and Metro International (in New York City), that serve international students and organize trips. As you get to know other students, you can plan trips together, but some people prefer the adventures of traveling alone. If you are organizing a trip with someone else, make sure you discuss finances, modes of transportation, and places to stay.

Just as anywhere else, it is important to "travel smart" in the U.S.

- *Pack lightly and do not bring valuables.*
- *Use traveler's checks, not cash.*
- *Use "street smarts" while exploring new places.*
- *Always let friends or family know where you will be at all times!*

If you want to travel inexpensively, look for youth hostels, located in many cities across the country. Hostelling International (http://www.hiayh.org/home.shtml) has over 125 hostel locations across the United States, from urban high-rise buildings with hundreds of beds to small hostels in rural settings. Camping is another inexpensive alternative, though you must purchase additional equipment such as a tent.

147

Going Home

Bryn Mawr College

Going Home **10**

PREPARING FOR A CAREER BACK HOME

It's never too early in the admissions process to start thinking about what you will do when it's time to go home. Careful planning before you leave your home country can help you make the most of your experience here and help you with a smooth transition home once your studies are complete.

It's a good idea before you leave home to do some research on professional careers in your country. What would you do with a degree from an American university? Why is it more desirable to get an American degree than one from your own country? What kind of employment will be available at home with your American degree?

Keep Up Contacts at Home

It's important to maintain contacts in your home country while you're studying in the United States.

- Does the school library carry a newspaper from your country? If not, is there a newsstand or book shop in town that does? It might be worth spending the money to arrange for an airmail subscription of your favorite newspaper.
- Are there international student organizations at your university? Meeting other students from your country is always a good way to keep up on news at home.

Make Contacts in the United States

The time you spend studying in the United States is invaluable for developing professional contacts. Do you plan to work in international finance? computer programming or engineering? Be sure to take advantage of the opportunities your university has to offer.

Perhaps you'd like to volunteer for a political organization. Maybe visiting an investment firm is more your style. Does your humanities college offer chances to work as a theater usher in exchange for a free Broadway show? Many do. These events are opportunities to network and make connections you can use later on.

Start a notebook containing potential professional contacts. Include the following information.

- The name of the company or organization
- A personal contact at the company
- The main phone number for the company and your personal contact's number
- The mailing address of the company
- A specific reference about how this person can help you

Once you're ready to start looking for a job back home, the people who have known you during the course of your American education will be an excellent source for employment leads, professional references, and job search tips.

After you finish your studies but before you depart the United States, contact all of these individuals and let them know that you are going home to find a job (or that you're looking for a job in the United States) and you would welcome their help or advice. Give them your contact information at home and take all of their contact information as well (phone and fax number, email address).

Creating and maintaining good business contacts is at the heart of the American professional community. The people you meet during your education can be the best contacts you ever have. Be sociable, get involved, and extend yourself. Use your time in the United States to get ahead back home.

Arrange Work Internships in Your Home Country

Many U.S. schools will ask you to participate in a professional internship as a requirement for your degree. This is a real opportunity for you. Most internships are partially or fully funded by the university and the sponsoring industry.

Since you are planning to work in your home country after you finish school, why not do your internship with a company at home? A three to six month internship in your home country will give you not only the opportunity to learn about your field of work, it will also give you the chance to meet people within the local business community. In other words, you can work for a stipend, gain professional experience, and create a network of contacts that will be helpful in your full-time job search after school.

Check with your university employment office, your academic advisor, and with American companies that have offices in other countries. Here are some useful Websites:

When you are ready to graduate, join the alumni association so that your school can maintain contact with you once you relocate. And if an alumni directory with addresses is available for purchase, buy it. It is a valuable resource to have.

International Internships
Maintained by the University of Denver, this is a very comprehensive and highly useful listing of international internships. Has direct links to hundreds of sites.
Website: http://www.du.edu/career/internetintintern.html

Council on International Educational Exchange (CIEE)
Website: http://www.councilexchanges.org

International Association for the Exchange of Students for Technical Experience
IASTE exchanges students from over 70 countries for practical training relevant to their studies.
Website: http://www.iaeste.org

International Job Listings
Well-organized and easy-to-use site maintained by Cornell University. Links to almost 50 sites.
Website: http://www.career.cornell.edu/students/search/international/intlTOC.html

Are You Ready to Start Looking for a Job?

1. Clarify your career goals and write a description of the ideal first job.

2. Design a résumé that targets your ideal job.

3. Get at least three letters of recommendation from previous employers and professors if possible. The letters should be one page in length, preferably on university or company letterhead paper, and they should be signed by the individuals who write the letters.

4. Identify the area of your university job placement service that focuses on your area of expertise (does the business school have its own placement office? The law school?). Meet with the job placement counselor there. Bring your résumé and your reference letters. A set of copies for the job placement service is acceptable. (Save the originals for your interviews.)

   Be honest and relaxed with your placement counselor. Try to be open to new possibilities, and don't say that you will accept a position that you honestly don't want. This is an informational meeting. Ask questions and take notes.

5. Keep a file of the employment suggestions (also called *leads*) you receive from your employment counselor. Keep in contact with her to let her know how things are progressing. That way, she can give you future referrals that are well suited to your needs.

Use the Job Placement Service at Your School

This is key. Almost every university has a job placement service. Many schools use the Internet to announce open positions. Your university job placement office is a free resource, and it can be very useful if you are prepared for and realistic about your goals.

PLAN YOUR JOB INTERVIEWS FROM THE UNITED STATES

Try to picture yourself in your dream job in your home country. What companies specialize in the job that you want? Is the company large or small? Is the job market strong? Would you like to work up to more senior positions in this company or will you get a few years of experience and move on to another company?

Write a Résumé or CV

Writing an effective résumé or CV is one of the most important steps you will take toward finding the job you want. But which format is best for you? In the United States, the résumé is the accepted standard when applying for a job. But in many Western European countries, the CV has long been the standard.

A *curriculum vitae (CV)* is a prose style summary of your personal and professional achievements. It contains information of a more biographical nature than the American-style résumé.

A *résumé* is a shorter, more concise syllabus of your professional accomplishments and education.

Many people include a career objective on their résumés, but this is optional. It's often difficult to define your objective before you have had much work experience. If you choose to include one, keep it specific to your profession and within realistic boundaries for the job you want.

A résumé contains employment and education-related information only. A CV contains more information about personal and professional goals. For example, a CV may contain your marital status, gender, and age. An American-style résumé would never contain this information. In fact, in many countries, including the United States, there are laws about what is considered "necessary information." Age, marital status, ethnicity, and gender all fall outside the boundaries of necessary information for an employer and so are not required on your résumé or CV. It may also be illegal for an employer to ask about these things in an interview in your home country. Ask others and find out before you start writing.

If your home country uses the CV more frequently than the résumé, that's what you need to write. It isn't necessary to write an American style résumé just because you've been studying in the United States. Alternatively, if your home country uses the résumé, compare the résumés you have seen at home to the résumés you see in the United States. How are their styles similar? Identify your potential employer and use the strongest parts of each style to write your résumé.

When it comes to presenting yourself to any potential employer through a résumé, less is more. In other words, *less information* (as long as it's strong and direct) is *more effective*. Try to keep a résumé to one page. Write in simple bullet points and keep your organization clean and easy to follow.

Joe Smith
1234 West Main, Apartment 200
Annapolis, MD 10000 USA
(304) 555-1212

Objective: Entry-level position in international finance analysis
[this line is optional]

Education:
1997   Columbia University, New York, NY, M.B.A., International Finance
1993   City University of New York, New York, NY, B.S., Business

Professional Experience:
1991–1992   Intern, UBS Securities (Swaps) Inc., New York, NY
     Review of master agreement documents
     Maintenance of daily P&L database input
     Tracking of confirmation status on deal terms

1990–1991   Assistant Manager, Happy's Ice Cream Shoppes, Annapolis, MD
     Staff scheduling
     Inventory control and ordering
     Customer service
     New employee training

Honors/Membership:
1995–1996   Solomon Brothers Presidential Scholar, Columbia University
1994–1995   President, Future Business Leaders of America,
     Columbia University
1993–present   Student Mentor, City Lights, Inc., New York, NY

Skills: Microsoft Word, Excel, and Claris Works for Macintosh and IBM

How to "Sell Yourself" on Paper

1. Use concrete language and avoid abstract words. To replace abstract language with more concrete words, ask yourself the following questions about your work experience: Who? What? When? Where? Why? How?

2. Use the active voice rather than the passive voice. That means writing sentences that explain what you have done, rather than what has been done to you.

3. Use graphics (but not too many). A properly designed résumé or CV draws the reader's eye to the most important information.

4. Be objective. If you were looking at your education and experience as an outsider might, how would you describe it? What are your strongest experiences? your weakest? What makes you unique? Remember, your potential interviewer has never met you before.

When writing a CV, the same rule follows: Less is more. Keep your CV specific to your professional experience. Write your CV in paragraph form, with vital biographical information at the top and professional and personal experience lower down.

Identifying Your Strengths and Weaknesses

Employers want to see your best side on your résumé or CV. They want to know who you are, what you've accomplished ,and what your professional goals are.

Some questions to ask yourself before you start writing your résumé are:

1. What were the key responsibilities of my previous jobs?

2. What qualities do they demonstrate? Managerial skills? Organizational skills? Technical skills? Creative skills?

In the United States, one very common interview question is, "What strengths and weaknesses do you have that would affect your ability to do this job?" Be honest, but try to turn it into a positive! Weaknesses are seen as "areas for growth" to a personnel department.

3. Which of these qualities match the responsibilities of the position I want?

4. What details of my work experience should I include? What should I omit?

5. What strengths does my American experience lend me?

6. What weaknesses does my American experience give me?

Organize your professional experience in reverse chronological order—with the most recent experience first, moving back in time to the job that is furthest in the past. Use the same rule for education: Most recent degree first, previous degree(s) following. If you are a recent graduate, list your education first on your résumé and your professional experience next with honors and technical skills at the bottom.

Once you have the résumé together, proofread! You don't want a simple typing error to hurt your chances of getting the perfect job.

Communicate with Prospective Employers

Keeping in touch with potential employers presents a special challenge for long-distance job hunters. Luckily, you have several options: email, fax, and overnight express service.

When you send your resume or CV to a potential employer, make sure you include a short *cover letter*. A cover letter is an introduction letter, where you state in just a few brief lines what position you are applying for. You should not go into great detail in your cover letter; that is the function of the résumé and CV.

The traditional resource for job postings (at least in the U.S.) is the newspaper classified advertising section. In the U.S., most new jobs are listed on Sunday. If you can locate a copy of the newspaper from your home country, read its classified ad section every week. And after you respond to an ad, keep a written record and follow up after a week or two, either by phone, fax, or mail.

Email: Almost every university will provide you with an email address and computer access for a small fee. Email allows you to send a cover letter with a résumé and letters of reference as electronic attachments. When you are investigating potential employers, find out their email address and keep it in your notebook.

Faxing: Once you have established a link with the company you want to work for, you might have to fax additional documents to support your application. If you send materials by fax, be sure to confirm that the transmission was received on the employer's side. You don't want to find out that the fax you sent was never received!

Overnight delivery services: If you have to send a package of materials that is too big to fax, or if you don't feel secure sending an electronic copy by email, use an express delivery service. Federal Express, Airborne Express, United Parcel Service, and even the U.S. Postal Service provide one- and two-day delivery service. This service is more expensive than regular mail, but it does provide fast service and security.

Regular mail: This is the least expensive and slowest mail service, but it is very reliable. You may want to find out how reliable the postal service is in your country, however. Do you really want to mail your master's thesis only to discover that the postal service in your country is on strike?

Interviewing

Interviewing is a lost art. If you have done your "homework" and have researched the company, an interview can be a rewarding experience. But if you have not prepared, it can be a terrible ordeal. Here are some tips to help you sparkle whether you are interviewing on the phone or in person.

1. Be prepared to expect any kind of interviewer. At some companies, you may be working with a professional personnel director. At others, you may be speaking to a department head or another employee who is not trained in interview techniques.

   The most important thing to establish with your interviewer is a personal connection. Be relaxed but respectful and try to put him at ease. Remember, the interviewer may be as nervous as you are. If he is well prepared, you won't have any troubles. If the interviewer does not ask about any information you want him to consider, he will probably give you an opportunity to volunteer this information. He might ask, "Is there anything you want to ask that we haven't talked about?" This is your chance. Be polite and succinct, but don't be afraid to let the interviewer know about any qualifications he or she may have missed.

   Make eye contact. Don't look at your shoes or your lap. Don't look at the bookshelf behind the interviewer's desk. Sit comfortably but in a businesslike manner in the chair. On a phone interview, don't interrupt but volunteer information whenever you're asked.

2. Learn about the company before the interview. What has the company done in the past? What are the company's goals now? How can you contribute to those goals? What experience or training do you have that will help the company attain its goals? How do the company's purposes mirror your professional aspirations?

   Try to help the interviewer see how, while the company is helping you, you will help the company as well.

3. Be honest! Don't fabricate experience or pretend that unacceptable responsibilities are "okay with you." You don't want to end up in a job that you're not qualified for, or one that you don't like. In an interview situation, honesty is your best policy.

4. Be respectful in your dress. Once you have learned about the company, you might have an idea of what kind of dress is acceptable in the office environment. Torn jeans and too much makeup are the wrong choice for an investment bank. Likewise, a plain blue suit and white shirt might be too conservative for a fashion magazine's editorial office. Wear a suit that shows a sense of style. Choose a dress that doesn't look too casual. Wear something that makes you look and feel terrific. Again, show interviewers your best, most professional side.

5. Follow up. Send a thank-you note to the interviewer(s) following the appointment. Offer to provide any further information the company may need in its decision-making process. About a week after the interview, check in with the personnel office to see how the search is progressing and to express your continued interest in the job.

6. Be prepared to answer questions, either subjective or objective. The following is a list of 10 questions that are frequently asked in interviews.

   • Why do you want to work at this company?

   • What are your strengths and weaknesses?

   • Tell me about yourself. (This is an open-ended question. The interviewer is interested in your professional experience and how it relates to the job. Try to keep your answer focused.)

   • Tell me about your employment experience.

   • Where do you see yourself in five years, ten years?

   • Do you have any interests or hobbies?

   • Can you organize yourself and manage your time to meet deadlines?

   • What do you expect to be paid? (Salary is generally not discussed at the first interview, so do not bring it up unless you're asked.)

- How would you best describe the job you are applying for?
- Do you have any questions about this company?

Use your interview and follow-up opportunities wisely. One of the primary reasons for an interview is to see how you respond in a tense situation. Are you cool and constructive, or nervous and nonproductive? If you follow these few simple rules, you'll be just fine.

LEAVING AMERICA

Once you have finished your education and are preparing to go home, you will have a lot to think about. Whether you have already found a job or you plan to conduct your employment search in your home country, leaving the United States and returning to your own culture will be a time of change.

Leaving the United States is not the end of your association with your university, your American contacts, or your American friends. In fact, it will be important to you in the years ahead to maintain the contacts you have made in this country.

As mentioned earlier, your university alumni association is an ideal organization to join. Not only can you get information on where your friends are and what's happening at your alma mater, but you can also list your own information with the alumni association so people can keep up with you. Many universities have alumni chapters in cities outside the university's location. Does your university have a chapter in your home country?

Your school or department within your university is also an ideal place to keep up contact. Don't forget to let your professors and advisors know where you are going and how they can contact you.

If you have been involved in community organizations or your local church, synagogue, or mosque, this is also a place to keep in touch. Keeping contact with friends in the community can help you stay connected to the United States beyond your university campus.

Before you leave the United States, you want to close up the details and as Americans say, "tie up all the loose ends."

Pre-Departure Checklist

❑ Arrange with the post office to have your mail forwarded to your new address

❑ Mail "change of address" postcards to all your friends and business contacts

❑ Disconnect your phone

❑ File for any outstanding medical coverage

❑ Pay off all outstanding debts, such as telephone or university services

❑ Close your bank account and/or transferred funds to your home country

❑ Purchase your plane tickets

❑ Purchase traveler's checks for your trip

❑ Sell any personal belongings you don't want to bring home

❑ Order copies of your school transcripts if you need them

❑ Receive your diploma or make arrangements to have it mailed to your new address

❑ Fill out your departure forms with the international office

❑ Check out of your apartment and return the key to the landlord

❑ Complete your customs and immigration documents

❑ Return any items you have borrowed

❑ Call the airline to ask about size and customs regulations for your suitcases

❑ Make arrangements for transportation to the airport and for someone to meet you when you arrive in your home country? (Remember to arrive at the airport at least two hours before your flight time.)

❑ Arrange to ship your items home, if necessary

Congratulations! You have completed your American degree, done some preparation for finding a new job, and made it home with the experience of a lifetime. You should be very proud of yourself. You have a great future ahead.

Resources

COMPREHENSIVE PROGRAMS AND SERVICES

U.S. Network for Education Information (USNEI)

Managed by the National Library of Education, this service provides official information for anyone seeking information about U.S. education. It is an extremely well-organized, easy-to-use site.

Phone: (202) 205-5019
Fax: (202) 401-0547
Website: http://www.ed.gov/NLE/USNEI/
Email: usnei@ed.gov

Institute for International Education (IIE)

IIE administers over 250 educational programs on behalf of sponsors that include foundations, corporations, government agencies, and international organizations. One new addition is AsiaJobSearch, an employment search service that links Asian graduates of U.S. schools with employers in East and Southeast Asia.

Phone: (212) 984-5400
Fax: (212) 984-5452
Website: http://www.iie.org/pgms/
(For international offices: http://www.iie.org/iie/osoffice.htm)

Edupass

Information on higher education in the United States.

Website: http://www.edupass.org

AMIDEAST

AMIDEAST provides extensive resources on U.S. study, scholarships, and training to the Middle Eastern and North African communities. Links to field offices in Egypt, Jordan, Kuwait, Lebanon, Morocco, Syria, Tunisia, the United Arab Emirates, the West Bank/Gaza Strip, and Yemen.

Phone: (202) 776-9600
Fax: (202) 776-7000
Website: http://www.amideast.org/programs/
Email: inquiries@amideast.org

College Board

The College Board is a nonprofit membership organization that provides guidance on college admissions, assessment, and financial aid. Its International Education Office has extensive information on programs for international students, and serves as a liaison between advisers worldwide and the international student offices of U.S. universities.

International Education Office/College Board
Phone: (202) 822-5900
Fax: (202) 822-5234
Website: http://www.collegeboard.org/ie/html/index000.html
Email: Internatl@collegeboard.org

The Fulbright Foundation

The Fulbright Program provides grants for graduate students, scholars and professionals, and teachers and administrators from the United States and other countries. Fulbright Binational Commissions are non-profit organizations that oversee the Fulbright Program abroad. Commissions propose annual country programs, which establish the numbers and categories of grants, based on requests from local institutions. There are currently 51 commissions worldwide.

Program overview
Website: http://exchanges.state.gov/education/fulbright/nonusflb.htm

List of commissions by country
Website: http://exchanges.state.gov/education/commiss.htm

ADMISSIONS TESTING

Many of the admissions tests are administered at various locations throughout the world. For an international test center near you, go to the test website or fax a request for information. Fees for each test range from approximately US $25 to 150.

TOEFL / TSE
Educational Testing Service/TOEFL Program
Phone: (609) 771-7100
Fax: (609) 771-7500
Website: http://www.toefl.org
Email: toefl@ets.org

For TOEFL representatives outside the United States:
http://www.toefl.org/repslist.html

SAT
College Board/SAT Program
Phone: (202) 822-5900
Fax: (202) 822-5920
Website: http://www.collegeboard.com
Email: sat@ets.org

ACT
ACT Inc.
Phone: (319) 337-1448
Fax: (319) 337-1285
Website: http://www.act.org/aap/regist/outside.html
Email: osus@act.org

GRE (Graduate Record Exam)
Educational Testing Service/GRE Program
Phone: (609) 771-7670
Fax: (609) 771-7906
Website: http://www.gre.org/atglance.html

To obtain test publications outside the United States:
http://www.ets.org/cbt/outsidus.html
Email: gre-info@ets.org

165

GMAT (Graduate Management Admission Test)
Educational Testing Service/GMAT Program
Phone: (609) 771-7330
Fax: (609) 883-4349
Website: http://www.gmat.org

To obtain test publications outside the United States:
http://www.ets.org/cbt/outsidus.html
Email: gmat@ets.org

MCAT (Medical College Admissions Test)
Phone: (319) 337-1357
Fax: (319) 337-1122
Website: http://www.aamc.org/students/mcat

LSAT (Law School Admission Test)
Phone: (215) 968-1001
Fax: (215) 968-1119
Website: http://www.lsac.org
Email: LSACinfo@LSAC.org

COLLEGE SEARCH

InfoUSA

Sponsored by U.S. government, this site provides a detailed introduction to the American system of higher education as well as practical information about study opportunities in the United States.

Website: http://usinfo.state.gov/usa/infousa/educ/studyus.htm

U.S. News & World Report Online: College and Careers

Sponsored by the newsmagazine *U.S. News & World Report*, this site provides comprehensive information on colleges and graduate schools, including a national ranking of schools and tools for helping you to estimate college costs.

Website: http://www.usnews.com/usnews/edu/eduhome.htm

NCES

Part of the U.S. Department of Education, the National Center for Education Statistics has a college search function where you can punch in the criteria you wish. It includes contact information and statistics for every school listed.

Website: http://nces.ed.gov/nceskids/college/

Yahoo! College Search

Direct access to all college websites arranged by state, as well as other higher education resources.

Website: http://dir.yahoo.com/Education/Higher_Education/

Web Central

Run by the University of Texas, this site offers direct internet access to accredited universities and community colleges organized by state.

Website: http://www.utexas.edu/world/univ/

Embark

This site is one of the most widely used for university-bound students. It has online applications to hundreds of leading undergraduate and undergraduate institutions, as well as profiles of many English language programs located in the United States.

Website: http://www.embark.com

JobWeb

Sponsored by the National Association of Colleges and Employers, this site contains many interesting articles and advice on a wide range of educational issues: school listings, often by academic discipline; careers; relocation costs; etc.

Website: http://www.jobweb.com/catapult/

EDUCATIONAL CONTACTS OUTSIDE THE UNITED STATES

U.S. Educational Advisers By Country
The Department of State provides support to a network of Educational Advising/Information Centers around the world. These centers advise prospective international students and other audiences on higher education and study opportunities in the United States.
Website: http://exchanges.state.gov/education/educationusa/asaeacs.htm

U.S. Embassies and Consulates Worldwide
Direct access to U.S. Embassies and Consulates listed by country
Website: http://travel.state.gov/links.html

U.S. Visa Services
This is the U.S. Department of State's official website for student visa information, including "What Consuls Look For."
Website: http://travel.state.gov/visa_services.html#niv

USEIC/Singapore
The official source information in Singapore on American higher education.
Phone: 65-226 6996
Fax: 65-223 0550
Website: http://useic.org/

SCHOLARSHIPS AND FINANCIAL AID

International Education Financial Aid
IEFA offers a searchable database of hundreds of scholarships and financial aid for international students wishing to study in a foreign country. Site includes detailed information and contact information for grants, scholarships, and loans for studying abroad.
Website: http://www.IEFA.org

FinAid
This is an excellent resource for financial aid available to international students.
Website: http://www.edupass.com/finaid/

International Funding Sources
An extensive list of hundreds of grants and scholarships available to international students.
Website: http://www.uiowa.edu/~vpr/research/sources/intfund.htm
Email: ann-donovan@uiowa.edu

Ford Foundation
The International Fellowships Program is a highly selective program which provides support for up to three years of graduate-level study to individuals from Africa, the Middle East, Asia, Latin America, and Russia.
Phone: (212) 573-5000
Fax: (212) 351-3677
Website: http://www.fordfound.org
Email: office-communications@fordfound.org

IREX
IREX is a nonprofit organization that administers programs between the United States and the countries of Eastern Europe, the New Independent States (NIS), Asia, and the Near East. Website lists many grant opportunities.
Website: http://www.irex.org/grants/index.htm
Email: irex@irex.org

Mobility International
This site offers information on financial aid specifically for students with disabilities.
Website: http://www.miusa.org/participant/finaid.html
Email: info@miusa.org

ENGLISH LANGUAGE PROGRAMS

Commission on English Language Program Accreditation (CEA)
CEA is a nonprofit corporation that accredits programs in English language across the country. On its website, it lists all accredited programs across the country.
Phone: (703) 518-2481
Fax: (703) 836-7864
Website: http://www.cea-accredit.org/
Email: ceakw@compuserve.com

The American Association of Intensive English Programs
The AAIEP website provides an extremely detailed program description of IEPs around the country. It includes detailed costs, class size, and class description.
Phone: (215) 895-5856
Fax: (215) 895-5854
Email: aaiep@drexel.edu
Website: http://www.aaiep.org

Glossary

Academic adviser is a member of a college faculty who advises students on academic matters.

Academic calendar is a schedule that lists the start and end dates for each academic term as well as all breaks, holidays, and important university deadlines. The academic calendar is usually September to May.

Academic probation is given to students who have fallen below an acceptable university grade point average (usually a C average). During this probation a student must raise his or her overall average by maintaining a minimum academic performance level.

Accident insurance is an insurance policy that pays part or all of any treatment for an injury due to accident.

Accredited refers to an institution that is certified by meeting certain a set of nationally recognized academic standards.

ACT is a standardized college entrance exam for undergraduate programs that is used in the college admissions process.

Admissions office is the office at a college or university that evaluates applications of undergraduate students to determine admission eligibility. Many admissions offices are also responsible for recruitment of new students.

Admissions requirements are the minimum academic qualifications that a candidate must have for admission to a university or college.

Advanced standing is the status given to transfer students who have earned more credits than a first-semester freshman before entering a college or universitty.

Affidavit of support is a form completed by a financial sponsor that guarantees financial support during a student's education.

Alumni organization is an organization made up of graduates from a certain university or college.

American Association of Intensive English Programs (AAIEP) is a board that, together with TESOL and the University Consortium of Intensive English Programs, has developed the core standards to ensure quality ESL instruction in intensive English programs.

Associate degree is a two-year degree (normally in a practical field) granted by community colleges and technical schools.

B-2 visa is a prospective student visa that is issued by the U.S. Immigration and Naturalization Service (INS) for a six-month period.

Bachelor's degree is a four-year degree granted by a university or college. The bachelor's degree is also called an *undergraduate degree.*

Bursar's office is the school office responsible for the money received for tuition and fees.

Campus security is a security service that operates on a university or college campus.

Certificate course is a specialized course leading to a certificate stating that the student has completed some coursework. Very often certificate courses are less than one year, and offered through the continuing education department of a college or university. See also *nondegree programs.*

Certified bank statement is a document issued by a bank that provides information on the financial assets of a student or a student's financial sponsor.

Chamber of Commerce is an association established to further the business interests of its community.

Class participation is the degree to which a student participates in class discussion periods by answering questions, posing questions, and giving and supporting opinions. In most university and college classes, this is a very important element in determining a student's grade. In some courses, class participation can count as much as 50 percent of the final grade.

College 1. a postsecondary academic institution that grants primarily bachelor's degrees 2. an academic or organizational unit within a university, e.g., the College of Liberal Arts. The word *college* is often used as a synonym for *university* without a distinction in meaning.

Community college is a postsecondary institution that mainly offers two-year programs and associate's degrees. A community college is also called a *junior college.*

Cost of living is the expense of living in a given city or area. For example, New York City has a higher cost of living than Ann Arbor, Michigan.

Credential is an educational document such as a transcript, degree, or diploma.

Credential evaluation is the formal review of a student's academic credentials for college admissions or placement.

Credits and **credit hours** are standardized measures of reporting college course completion, the most common of which is the semester credit hour. Students usually complete 30–32 semester credits in an academic year. Schools following the quarter system require the completion of approximately 15 quarter hours per semester or 45 quarter hour credits per academic year.

Cultural Affairs Office of the U.S. Embassy is the office charged with matters of culture, including educational advisement for international students planning on coming to the United States for study.

Culture shock is the psychological response people have to entering a new culture.

Curriculum is a fixed series of courses offered in a college program leading to a degree or certificate.

Curriculum vitae (CV) is a brief document listing a person's educational and professional experiences that is used to determine his or her suitability for employment. See *résumé*.

Deadline dates are dates on or before which documents for admission (or another administrative or academic function) must be received by a school.

Degree is an academic credential given to a student after completing a required course of study. See *bachelor's degree, master's degree, Ph.D.*

Diploma is a certificate awarded to a student by a school, college, or university. It indicates graduation from the institution or the granting of a degree.

Distribution requirements are the class requirements that undergraduate students must take outside of their specific major. These classes are meant to give students a working knowledge of several different disciplines. Also called *liberal arts requirements*.

Doctoral candidate is a student accepted into a doctoral program and working towards the completion of a Ph.D. or other doctorate degree.

Dissertation is an independent and original scholarly work prepared by a student in partial fulfillment for the doctorate degree.

Doctorate degree is the degree of doctor conferred by a university. Doctorate is used primarily to refer to the Ph.D.

Dormitory is a housing unit on the campus of a university or college where enrolled students live. Most dormitories have a cafeteria where the students have their meals. See *room and board*.

Double major is a course of study in which a student works for and completes the requirements of two independent majors.

Drop/add In American universities and colleges, students may drop and add courses before certain deadlines which are published in the institution's academic calendar.

Electives are courses not required for a student's major but taken by students out of interest or to fulfill credits for graduation.

Elementary school is a school for grades 1 through 6 in the U.S. school system. Also called *grammar school.*

Employment recruiters are representatives from businesses and organizations whose job it is to seek out employment candidates from among college seniors.

English proficiency requirements Virtually all schools require for admissions that students whose first language is not English prove that they have attained a certain level of English proficiency.

Exchange programs are offered through a university or college and allow American students to travel and live abroad, usually studying language and/or culture at a foreign university. Exchange programs may also offer studying opportunities in the university for international students to come to the United States for a certain amount of time.

F-1 visa is a student visa issued for a student's duration of study in the United States.

Fees are school charges for services such as the library, athletic activities, and health services. International students are required to pay fees as well as tuition. There may also be an additional mandatory health insurance fee.

Final exam is the last examination given in the course, and is usually, but not always, of a comprehensive nature. Normally, a final exam is weighed more in the computation of the final grade than are the other tests given throughout the course.

Financial aid is money for studying and living that is made available by an organization or person outside of the student's immediate family. Financial aid may be in the form of a bank loan or a graduate research or teaching assistantship.

Financial documentation is proof, usually in the form of a bank statement, that a student has sufficient funding for studies in the United States. Financial documentation is required for a college or university to issue an I-20.

Foreign student services are services provided by the international office that are specifically for students from other countries. Typical services are visa assistance and international student orientation.

Four-point scale is a grading system in which a letter grade (A, B, C, D, and F) is assigned a numerical value (4, 3, 2, 1, and 0, respectively). A student is then ranked according to an average of all of her course work. For example, if a student receives an A, a B, and two Cs, then his or her rank on a four-point scale would be 2.75. This rank is also referred to as a *GPA* (grade-point average).

Fraternity is a college organization of men represented by a Greek letter. See *Greek system.*

Freshman is a student in the first year of high school or college.

Full-time student is a student who carries a number of credit hours within a semester set by the college or university as being full time. All students with an F-1 student visa must be enrolled as a full-time students. For most schools, full time is 12 credit hours per semester.

General education requirements see *distribution requirements.*

GMAT (Graduate Management Admissions Test) is the aptitude test taken for admission into most graduate business (M.B.A.) programs.

Grade Point Average (GPA) is the numerical ranking of a student based on his or her average grade performance. See *four-point scale.*

Graduate school is 1. academic study beyond the bachelor's degree leading to a graduate degree such as the master's or doctorate. 2. the academic division at a university charged with administering the school's graduate programs.

Graduate degree is a higher degrees beyond the bachelor's degree, such as the master's or doctorate.

Graduate student is a student who has already gained at least a bachelor's degree and is working toward an advanced degree.

GRE (Graduate Record Examination) is the aptitude test used for admission into most master's and doctoral programs.

Greek system refers to sorority or fraternity student clubs affiliated with a university and identified under a combination of Greek letters. Such clubs usually have their own residence and social events.

Health insurance see *accident insurance.*

Health services are medical and pharmaceutical services that are offered to enrolled students at a college or university. Services generally include physician appointments, prescriptions, and alcohol and drug abuse awareness seminars.

High school is a school for grades 9 through 12 (usually ages 14 through 18) in the U.S. school system.

Housing office is the school office responsible for placing students into dormitories on campus.

Humanities are the branches of learning concerned with human thought and relations, as distinguished from the sciences. Humanities includes literature, philosophy, fine arts, and history.

I–20 is the documentation issued by a U.S. school that allows an international student to solicit an F-1 visa.

I–515 is a replacement document for the I-20 obtainable before entering the United States. Even with this document a student has only a month to get a new I-20.

I–94 is a document stapled to the inside of the passport, showing a visitor's visa status.

Intensive English Programs (IEPs) are programs that specialize in the intensive teaching of the English language to speakers of other languages. Such programs may be proprietary (privately owned and operated) or they may be departments within a university. IEPs vary in terms of quality and variety of offerings.

Interdisciplinary studies are special programs that integrate course work from several different university programs in order to focus on a range of topics. Recently, many universities and colleges have begun to arrange cultural studies under this type of model.

Internship is a position for a fixed time in which a student (or graduate) works for some company or organization in a field related to his or her major.

International Student Advisor is the person at the school responsible for advising incoming international students. This person will usually issue the I-20 documentation or other types of visa assistance and give newcomer orientations for international students.

Ivy League refers to a group of colleges in the northeastern United States known for excellent academic programs.

J–1 is an exchange visitor's visa.

J.D. is a professional degree in law.

Junior college See *community college.*

Junior high school is a school for grades 7 and 8 in the U.S. school system.

Junior is a student in the third year of high school or college.

Lab fees are additional fees charged to students for classes that require work in a laboratory. See *fees.*

Land grant colleges and land grant universities are colleges or universities built on land appropriated by a state government for that purpose. These schools are often referred to synonymously with state colleges and universities.

Letter grade is a grading system that assigns a letter (A = superior, B = above average, C = average, F = fail) to score a student's performance in a given class.

Liberal arts see *humanities.*

Lower division generally refers to the first two years of work towards a bachelor's degree.

Law School Admissions Test (LSAT) is the aptitude test used as one of the factors to determine a candidate's eligibility into law school.

M-1 is a visa issued to an international student who will be pursuing studies at a vocational or recognized nonacademic institution.

M.D. is a professional degree in medicine.

Major is a student's primary course of study at a university or college. The major a student chooses determines the type of distribution requirements (see above) a student must complete as well as the type of degree a student will receive after graduating.

Master's degree is a degree given in a college or university to a person who has completed a prescribed course of graduate study in the humanities (Master of Arts) or sciences (Master of Sciences).

Master's thesis is an independent scholarly work prepared by a student in partial fulfillment for the master's degree.

Master's in Business Administration (M.B.A.) is the advanced degree awarded to a person graduating from a business school.

Medical College Admissions Test (MCAT) is the aptitude test used as one of the factors to determine a candidate's eligibility into medical school.

Master's in Fine Arts (M.F.A.) is a graduate degree in writing, painting, sculpting, music, theater, or dance.

Midterm is an exam given halfway through the completion of a course. Midterm exams may be specific to a certain course issue or comprehensive.

Minor is a student's secondary course of study at a university or college.

Money order is a check for a specified sum of money, usually purchased at a post office or bank and used for the payment of some service. Most institutions will ask for a money order or personal check when paying by mail.

Nondegree program is a program at a college or university that does not lead to a degree. See certificate programs.

Nonimmigrant status is one of several visa status designations that allow noncitizens to remain in the United States for a definite period of time.

Off-campus refers to student activities and housing that are not on the campus itself. The term, however, does not necessarily imply a lack of university sponsorship, although it often does.

On-campus refers to student activities and housing that are on the campus itself. The term implies university sponsorship.

Orientation week is a special week set aside for the orientation of students new to a campus. Different types of orientations are held for freshman students, international students, and graduate students.

Part-time student is a student who carries fewer than the minimum number of credit hours within a semester set by the college or university for full-time status. Generally, students on an F-1 visa may not be part time.

Pass/fail Some courses are offered on a pass/fail basis, meaning that students do not receive grades but rather a P for pass or an F for fail. Pass/fail scores are not usually computed in the GPA.

Personal essay is an essay or personal statement required on most applications. The essay demonstrates why the candidate would be a desirable student for the university and/or program.

Ph.D. is the degree or status of doctor that is conferred by a university to a student who has completed the doctoral-level course work in some field of education.

Postdoctoral fellows or "postdocs" Many colleges and universities offer recently graduated doctoral students (see Ph.D.) a limited time on the campus to do research and/or teach. Postdocs may or may not receive a salary.

Prerequisites are courses that a student is required to complete in order to be eligible for a more advanced course.

Quarter is a period of study at a university or college usually from 8–10 weeks. See also *semester*.

Recommendations or reference letters are letters written by a student's former teachers and/or professional colleagues stating why she is a good candidate for admission into a university program.

Registration is enrollment into a set of classes for a quarter or a semester.

Registrar's office is the office on the campus responsible for maintaining students' records of enrollment and establishing enrollment procedures and policies.

Research assistantship is a position given to a graduate student requiring a specific number of hours of work per week on a research project that the department oversees. Research assistantships generally carry a financial stipend.

Resident Assistant (RA) is a student given the responsibility of providing assistance to students living in a school dormitory. An RA is generally a junior or senior student who lives at the dormitory.

Résumé is a brief document listing a person's educational and professional experiences. It is used to determine whether an applicant is a good candidate for a given job position.

Room and board is the combination of housing and meals in a leasing agreement.

Roommate is a person with whom one shares housing. Most roommate situations involve the sharing of rent and utility expenses but not personal toiletries or food.

Safety school is a school to which an applicant is highly confident he will be admitted.

SAT exam is the standardized college admissions test for undergraduate programs.

Scholarship is a financial award based on merit, including outstanding academic performance. The term is often used interchangebly with "financial aid."

Sealed envelope is an envelope that has been sealed and signed across the back flap to ensure that no one except the sender has seen the contents. Most universities and colleges ask that a student's recommendations be sent in a sealed envelope.

Semester is a period of study at a university or college, usually from 16–18 weeks. See also *quarter*.

Senior is a student in the fourth year of high school or college.

Sophomore is a student in the second year of high school or college.

Sorority is a college organization of women. The name of a sorority is usually represented by Greek letters. See *Greek system*.

Stretch school (or reach school) is a school to which an applicant is not sure or doubtful of admission.

Students with disabilities are students who have physical or learning disabilities that require specially equipped space (such as a wheelchair ramp) or special learning services (such as untimed examinations). Most colleges or universities have offices that specifically support these students.

Student union is the building on campus that houses student services.

Summer school is an academic session held during summer break. Since there is less time, classes held in the summer are more intensive than those held during the regular semester.

Syllabus is an outline of topics and readings that will be covered in a course.

Teaching assistant is a graduate student who assists in teaching an undergraduate course. Teaching assistants generally receive a modest payment.

Technical school is a postsecondary institution that offers certificates or associate degrees in technical fields such as auto mechanics.

Tenured professor is a professor who has been awarded his university position for life. A professor who has tenure cannot be dismissed.

TESOL refers to 1. the Teaching of English to Speakers of Other Languages 2. the professional association of Teachers of English to Speakers of Other Languages.

TOEFL (Test of English as a Foreign Language) is an English proficiency exam required of appicants whose native language is not English.

Transcripts are the official documents compiled by a school that detail a student's academic courses and grades.

Transfer The process of moving from one school to another school.

Tuition is the cost of instruction at a school.

Tutorial services are services provided by the university that offer students extra help in an area of difficulty. For example, most universities offer writing labs where students can go for help in writing essays and research papers.

Undeclared major refers to a student's status while he or she is deciding which major field of study to select.

Undergraduate student is a college or university student working toward a bachelor's degree.

University and College Intensive English Programs (UCIEP) is a board that, together with TESOL and AAIEP, has developed core standards to ensure quality ESL instruction in intensive English programs.

University is a large postsecondary institution for higher learning consisting of several colleges that grant bachelor's, master's, and doctorate degrees. See *college*.

Upper division generally refers to the last two years of study toward a bachelor's degree.

Vacation period are periods when classes are not in session and university campuses are closed. The most popular vacation periods are: Christmas break (late December through early January), spring break (one week in March), Thanksgiving (several days in late November), and intersession breaks (late May and early August).

Visa Waiver Program is an international agreement that allows visitors from certain countries to come to the United States without a visa. Instead, the passport is marked W/T and the visitor may stay in the United States for 90 days. W/T status may not be changed for any other visa status.

180

School Websites

Following is a list of website addresses for many U.S. colleges and universities. Because of space limitations, the list is comprehensive though not complete. For the precise location of individual states, please refer to the map of the United States at the front of this book.

Alabama

Alabama State University
http://www.alasu.edu

Troy State University
http://www.troyst.edu

Tuskegee University
http://www.tusk.edu

University of Alabama
http://www.ua.edu

University of Alabama—Birmingham
http://www.uab.edu

University of Alabama—Huntsville
http://www.uah.edu

University of North Alabama
http://www.una.edu

Alaska

University of Alaska—Anchorage
http://www.uaa.alaska.edu

University of Alaska—Fairbanks
http://www.uaf.edu

Arizona

Arizona State University
http://www.asu.edu

Embry-Riddle Aeronautical
University—Arizona
http://www.pr.erau.edu

Northern Arizona University
http://www.nau.edu

University of Arizona
http://www.arizona.edu

Western International University
http://www.wintu.edu

Arkansas

Arkansas State University
http://www.astate.edu

Arkansas Tech University
http://www.atu.edu

Henderson State University
http://www.hsu.edu

Southern Arkansas University
http://www.saumag.edu

University of Arkansas—Little Rock
http://www.ualr.edu

California

Academy of Art College
http://www.academyart.edu

Art Center College of Design
http://www.artcenter.edu

California College of Arts and Crafts
http://www.ccac-art.edu

California Institute of Technology
http://www.caltech.edu

California Institute of the Arts
http://www.calarts.edu

California State Polytechnic
University—Pomona
http://www.csupomona.edu

California State University—Long Beach
http://www.csulb.edu

California State University—Los Angeles
http://www.calstatela.edu

Golden Gate University
http://www.ggu.edu

La Sierra University
http://www.lasierra.edu

California (cont.)

Loyola Marymount University
http://www.lmu.edu

Occidental College
http://www.oxy.edu

Pacific Union College
http://www.puc.edu

Pepperdine University
http://www.pepperdine.edu

Pitzer College
http://www.pitzer.edu

Pomona College
http://www.pomona.edu

San Diego State University
http://www.sdsu.edu

San Francisco State University
http://www.sfsu.edu

San Jose State University
http://www.sjsu.edu

Santa Clara University
http://www.scu.edu

Stanford University
http://www.stanford.edu

United States International University
http://www.usiu.edu

University of California—Berkeley
http://www.berkeley.edu

University of California—San Diego
http://www.ucsd.edu

University of San Diego
http://www.sandiego.edu

University of San Francisco
http://www.usfca.edu

University of Southern California
http://www.usc.edu

University of the Pacific
http://www.uop.edu

Whittier College
http://www.whittier.edu

Colorado

Colorado College
http://www.ColoradoCollege.edu

Colorado School of Mines
http://www.mines.edu

University of Colorado—Denver
http://www.cudenver.edu

University of Denver
http://www.du.edu

Western State College of Colorado
http://www.western.edu

Connecticut

Connecticut College
http://www.conncoll.edu

University of Bridgeport
http://www.bridgeport.edu

University of Hartford
http://www.hartford.edu

University of New Haven
http://www.newhaven.edu

Wesleyan University
http://www.wesleyan.edu

Yale University
http://www.yale.edu

Delaware

Delaware State University
http://www.dsc.edu

University of Delaware
http://www.udel.edu

District of Columbia

American University
http://www.american.edu

Catholic University of America
http://www.cua.edu

George Washington University
http://www.gwu.edu

Georgetown University
http://www.georgetown.edu/

Howard University
http://www.howard.edu

Florida

Barry University
http://www.barry.edu

Eckerd College
http://www.eckerd.edu

Embry-Riddle Aeronautical University—Florida
http://www.embryriddle.edu

Florida Atlantic University
http://www.fau.edu

Florida Institute of Technology
http://www.fit.edu

Florida State University
http://www.fsu.edu

Honors College of Florida Atlantic
University
http://www.honorscollege.edu

Lynn University
http://www.lynn.edu

Nova Southeastern University
http://www.nova.edu

Saint Thomas University
http://www.stu.edu

Schiller International University
http://www.schiller.edu

University of Miami
http://www.miami.edu

University of Tampa
http://www.utampa.edu

Georgia

Emory University
http://www.www.emory.edu

Georgia Institute of Technology
http://www.gatech.edu

Georgia State University
http://www.gsu.edu

Mercer University
http://www.mercer.edu

Morehouse College
http://www.morehouse.edu

Savannah College of Art and Design
http://www.scad.edu

Southern Polytechnic State University
http://www.spsu.edu

University of Georgia
http://www.uga.edu

Wesleyan College
http://www.wesleyancollege.edu

Hawaii

Brigham Young University—Hawaii
http://www.byuh.edu

Hawaii Pacific University
http://www.hpu.edu

Idaho

Lewis-Clark State College
http://www.lcsc.edu

University of Idaho
http://www.its.uidaho.edu/
uihome

Illinois

Benedictine University
http://www.ben.edu

Columbia College—Chicago
http://www.colum.edu

DePaul University
http://www.depaul.edu

Illinois Institute of Technology
http://www.iit.edu

Knox College
http://www.knox.edu

Lake Forest College
http://www.lakeforest.edu

Monmouth College
http://www.monm.edu

Northwestern University
http://www.northwestern.edu

School of the Art Institute of Chicago
http://www.artic.edu/saic

University of Chicago
http://www.uchicago.edu

University of Illinois—Chicago
http://www.uic.edu

University of Illinois—Urbana-
Champaign
http://www.uiuc.edu

Indiana

Earlham College
http://www.earlham.edu

Hanover College
http://www.hanover.edu

Indiana Institute of Technology
http://www.indtech.edu

Purdue University—West Lafayette
http://www.purdue.edu

Tri-State University
http://www.www.tristate.edu

University of Indianapolis
http://www.uindy.edu

Indiana (cont.)

University of Notre Dame
http://www.nd.edu

Valparaiso University
http://www.valpo.edu

Wabash College
http://www.wabash.edu

Iowa

Drake University
http://www.drake.edu

Grinnell College
http://www.grinnell.edu

Iowa State University
http://www.iastate.edu

Simpson College
http://www.simpson.edu

University of Dubuque
http://www.dbq.edu

University of Iowa
http://www.uiowa.edu

Kansas

Bethel College
http://www.bethelks.edu

University of Kansas
http://www.ku.edu

Wichita State University
http://www.wichita.edu

Kentucky

Murray State University
http://www.murraystate.edu

University of Kentucky
http://www.uky.edu

University of Louisville
http://www.louisville.edu

Louisiana

Louisiana State University and A&M College
http://www.lsu.edu

Southern University and A&M College
http://www.subr.edu

Tulane University
http://www.tulane.edu

University of New Orleans
http://www.uno.edu

Maine

Bates College
http://www.bates.edu

Bowdoin College
http://www.bowdoin.edu

Colby College
http://www.colby.edu

College of the Atlantic
http://www.coa.edu

University of Maine
http://www.umaine.edu

University of Maine at Machias
http://www.umm.maine.edu

University of New England
http://www.une.edu

Maryland

Goucher College
http://www.goucher.edu

Hood College
http://www.hood.edu

Johns Hopkins University
http://www.jhu.edu

Maryland Institute—College of Art
http://www.mica.edu

St. John's College
http://www.sjca.edu

Towson University
http://www.towson.edu

University of Maryland—Baltimore County
http://www.umbc.edu

University of Maryland—College Park
http://www.maryland.edu

University of Maryland—Eastern Shore
http://www.umd.edu

Washington College
http://www.washcoll.edu

Western Maryland College
http://www.wmdc.edu

Massachusetts

American International College
http:// www.aic.edu

Amherst College
http://www.amherst.edu

Babson College
http://www.babson.edu

Bentley College
http://www.bentley.edu

Berklee College of Music
http://www.berklee.edu

Boston College
http://www.bc.edu

Boston Conservatory
http://www.bostonconservatory.edu

Boston University
http://www.bu.edu

Brandeis University
http://www.brandeis.edu

Clark University
http://www.clarku.edu

Emerson College
http://www.emerson.edu

Emmanuel College
http://www.emmanuel.edu

Framingham State College
http://www.framingham.edu

Hampshire College
http://www.hampshire.edu

Harvard College
http://www.fas.harvard.edu

Lesley College
http://www.lesley.edu

Massachusetts College of Art
http://www.massart.edu

Massachusetts College of Pharmacy
and Allied Health Sciences
http://www.mcp.edu

Massachusetts Institute of Technology
http://www.mit.edu

Massachusetts Maritime Academy
http://www.mma.mass.edu

Mount Holyoke College
http://www.mtholyoke.edu

New England Conservatory of Music
http://www.newengland
conservatory.edu

Northeastern University
http://www.neu.edu

Pine Manor College
http://www.pmc.edu

Regis College
http://www.regiscollege.edu

Simmons College
http://www.simmons.edu

Smith College
http://www.smith.edu

Springfield College
http://www.spfldcol.edu

Suffolk University
http://www.suffolk.edu

Tufts University
http://www.tufts.edu

University of Massachusetts—Amherst
http://www.umass.edu

University of Massachusetts—Boston
http://www.umb.edu

Wellesley College
http://www.wellesley.edu

Wentworth Institute of Technology
http://www.wit.edu

Wheaton College
http://www.wheatoncollege.edu

Williams College
http://www.williams.edu

Worcester Polytechnic Institute
http://www.wpi.edu

Michigan

Calvin College
http://www.calvin.edu

Eastern Michigan University
http://www.emich.edu

Ferris State University
http://www.ferris.edu

Kettering University
http://www.kettering.edu

Lake Superior State University
http://www.lssu.edu

Michigan State University
http://www.msu.edu

Michigan Technological University
http://www.mtu.edu

Saginaw Valley State University
http://www.svsu.edu

University of Michigan—Ann Arbor
http://www.umich.edu

Wayne State University
http://www.wayne.edu

Western Michigan University
http://www.wmich.edu

Minnesota

Macalester College
http://www.macalester.edu

Minnesota State University—Mankato
http://www.mnsu.edu

Saint Cloud State University
http://www.stcloudstate.edu

University of Minnesota—Twin Cities
http://www.umn.edu/tc/

Mississippi

Rust College
http://www.rustcollege.edu

University of Mississippi
http://www.olemiss.edu

University of Southern Mississippi
http://www.usm.edu

Missouri

Central Missouri State University
http://www.cmsu.edu

Columbia College
http://www.ccis.edu

Lindenwood College
http://www.lindenwood.edu

Maryville University of Saint Louis
http://www.maryville.edu

Saint Louis University
http://www.imagine.slu.edu

Truman State University
http://www.truman.edu

University of Missouri—Columbia
http://www.missouri.edu

University of Missouri—Kansas City
http://www.umkc.edu

University of Missouri—St. Louis
http://www.umsl.edu/
admissions/admission.html

Washington University in St. Louis
http://www.wustl.edu

Webster University
http://www.webster.edu/
webmain2.html

Montana

Montana State University
http://www.montana.edu

University of Montana—Missoula
http://www.umt.edu

Nebraska

Bellevue University
http://www.bellevue.edu

Creighton University
http://www.creighton.edu

University of Nebraska—Kearney
http://www.unk.edu

University of Nebraska—Lincoln
http://www.unl.edu

University of Nebraska—Omaha
http://www.unomaha.edu

Wayne State College
http://www.wsc.edu

Nevada

University of Nevada—Las Vegas
http://www.unlv.edu

University of Nevada—Reno
http://www.unr.edu

New Hampshire

Dartmouth College
http://www.dartmouth.edu

New Hampshire College
http://www.nhc.edu

University of New Hampshire
http://www.unh.edu

New Jersey

Drew University
http://www.drew.edu

Fairleigh Dickinson University
http://www.fdu.edu

Montclair State University
http://www.montclair.edu

New Jersey City University
http://www.njcu.edu

New Jersey Institute of Technology
http://www.njit.edu

Princeton University
http://www.princeton.edu

Ramapo College of New Jersey
http://www.ramapo.edu

Rider University
http://www.rider.edu

Rutgers University
http://www.rutgers.edu

Seton Hall University
http://www.shu.edu

Stevens Institute of Technology
http://www.stevens-tech.edu

New Mexico

University of New Mexico
http://www.unm.edu

New York

Adelphi University
http://www.adelphi.edu

Albany College of Pharmacy
http://www.acp.edu

Alfred University
http://www.alfred.edu

Bard College
http://www.bard.edu

Barnard College
http://www.barnard.edu

Canisius College
http://www.canisius.edu

City University of New York—Baruch College
http://www.baruch.cuny.edu

City University of New York—Brooklyn College
http://www.brooklyn.cuny.edu

City University of New York—City College
http://www.ccny.cuny.edu

City University of New York—College of Staten Island
http://www.csi.cuny.edu

City University of New York—Hunter College
http://www.hunter.cuny.edu

City University of New York—John Jay College of Criminal Justice
http://www.jjay.cuny.edu

City University of New York—Lehman College
http://www.lehman.edu

City University of New York—Medgar Evers College
http://www.mec.cuny.edu

City University of New York—Queens College
http://www.qc.edu

City University of New York—York College
http://www.york.cuny.edu

Clarkson University
http://www.clarkson.edu

Colgate University
http://www.colgate.edu

College of Mount Saint Vincent
http://www.cmsv.edu

College of New Rochelle—The School of Arts and Sciences and The School of Nursing
http://www.cnr.edu

Columbia University—Columbia College
http://www.columbia.edu

Columbia University—Foundation School of Engineering and Applied Science
http://www.columbia.edu

Columbia University—School of GeneralStudies
http://www.gs.columbia.edu

Cooper Union for the Advancement of Science and Art
http://www.cooper.edu

Cornell University
http://www.cornell.edu

D'Youville College
http://www.dyc.edu

Eugene Lang College
http://www.newschool.edu

Fordham University
http://www.fordham.edu

Hamilton College
http://www.hamilton.edu

Hartwick College
http://www.hartwick.edu

Hofstra University
http://www.hofstra.edu

New York (cont.)

Houghton College
http://www.houghton.edu

Iona College
http://www.iona.edu

Ithaca College
http://www.ithaca.edu

Juilliard School
http://www.juilliard.edu

Long Island University
http://www.liu.edu

Manhattan College
http://www.manhattan.edu

Manhattanville College
http://www.mville.edu

Mannes College of Music
http://www.mannes.edu

Marymount Manhattan College
http://www.marymount.
mmm.edu/home.htm

New York Institute of Technology—
Old Westbury
http://www.nyit.edu

New York University
http://www.nyu.edu

Niagara University
http://www.niagara.edu

Nyack College
http://www.nyackcollege.edu

Pace University—New York
http://www.pace.edu

Parsons School of Design
http://www.parsons.edu

Polytechnic University
http://www.poly.edu

Pratt Institute
http://www.pratt.edu

Rensselaer Polytechnic Institute
http://www.rpi.edu

Rochester Institute of Technology
http://www.rit.edu

Saint Francis College
http://www.stfranciscollege.edu

Saint John's University
http://www.stjohns.edu

Sarah Lawrence College
http://www.sarahlawrence.edu

School of Visual Arts
http://www.schoolofvisual
arts.edu

Skidmore College
http://www.skidmore.edu

St. Lawrence University
http://www.stlawu.edu

State University of New York
http://www.suny.edu

Syracuse University
http://www.syracuse.edu

Union College
http://www.union.edu

University of Rochester
http://www.rochester.edu

Vassar College
http://www.vassar.edu

Wagner College
http://www.wagner.edu

Yeshiva University
http://www.yu.edu

North Carolina

Barton College
http://www.barton.edu

Campbell University
http://www.campbell.edu/
cuindex.html

Duke University
http://www.duke.edu

Lees-McRae College
http://www.lmc.edu

North Carolina School of the Arts
http://www.ncarts.edu

Pfeiffer University
http://www.pfeiffer.edu

Queens College
http://www.queens.edu

Salem College
http://www.salem.edu

University of North Carolina—Asheville
http://www.unca.edu

University of North Carolina—
Chapel Hill
http://www.unc.edu

University of North Carolina—Charlotte
http://www.uncc.edu

University of North Carolina—
Wilmington
http://www.uncwil.edu

Wake Forest University
http://www.wfu.edu

Winston-Salem State University
http://www.wssu.edu

North Dakota

Minot State University
http://www.misu.nodak.edu

North Dakota State University
http://www.ndsu.edu

University of North Dakota
http://www.und.edu

Ohio

Case Western Reserve University
http://www.cwru.edu

College of Wooster
http://www.wooster.edu

Denison University
http://www.denison.edu

Franklin University
http://www.franklin.edu

Kent State University
http://www.kent.edu

Kenyon College
http://www.kenyon.edu

Marietta College
http://www.marietta.edu

Oberlin College
http://www.oberlin.edu

Ohio Dominican College
http://www.odc.edu

Ohio State University
http://www.osu.edu

Ohio University
http://www.ohiou.edu

Ohio Wesleyan University
http://www.owu.edu

Wittenberg University
http://www.wittenberg.edu

Oklahoma

Oklahoma State University
http://www.okstate.edu

University of Central Oklahoma
http://www.ucok.edu

University of Oklahoma
http://www.ou.edu

University of Science and Arts of Oklahoma
http://www.usao.edu

University of Tulsa
http://www.utulsa.edu

Oregon

Eastern Oregon University
http://www.eou.edu

Lewis and Clark College
http://www.lclark.edu

Oregon Institute of Technology
http://www.oit.edu

Oregon State University
http://www.oregonstate.edu

Portland State University
http://www.pdx.edu

University of Oregon
http://www.uoregon.edu

University of Portland
http://www.up.edu

Pennsylvania

Albright College
http://www.alb.edu

Bryn Mawr College
http://www.brynmawr.edu

Bucknell University
http://www.bucknell.edu/

Carnegie Mellon University
http://www.cmu.edu

Clarion University of Pennsylvania
http://www.clarion.edu

Drexel University
http://www.drexel.edu

Duquesne University
http://www.duq.edu

Franklin and Marshall College
http://www.fandm.edu

Pennsylvania (cont.)

Haverford College
http://www.haverford.edu

Indiana University of Pennsylvania
http://www.iup.edu

La Salle University
http://www.lasalle.edu

Lafayette College
http://www.lafayette.edu

Lehigh University
http://www.lehigh.edu

Mansfield University
http://www.mansfield.edu

Mercyhurst College
http://www.mercyhurst.edu

Messiah College
http://www.messiah.edu

Moore College of Art and Design
http://www.moore.edu

Pennsylvania State University—
University Park
http://www.psu.edu

Philadelphia University
http://www.PhilaU.edu

Point Park College
http://www.ppc.edu

Saint Joseph's University
http://www.sju.edu

Slippery Rock University
http://www.sru.edu

Swarthmore College
http://www.swarthmore.edu

Temple University
http://www.temple.edu

University of Pennsylvania
http://www.upenn.edu

University of Pittsburgh
http://www.pitt.edu

University of the Arts
http://www.uarts.edu

Villanova University
http://www.villanova.edu

Washington and Jefferson College
http://www.washjeff.edu

Rhode Island

Brown University
http://www.brown.edu

Bryant College
http://www.bryant.edu

Johnson & Wales University
http://www.jwu.edu

Providence College
http://www.providence.edu

Rhode Island College
http://www.ric.edu

Rhode Island School of Design
http://www.risd.edu

Roger Williams University
http://www.rwu.edu

University of Rhode Island
http://www.uri.edu

South Carolina

Citadel
http://www.citadel.edu

Coastal Carolina University
http://www.coastal.edu

College of Charleston
http://www.cofc.edu

Francis Marion University
http://www.fmarion.edu

University of South Carolina
http://www.sc.edu

Winthrop University
http://www.winthrop.edu

South Dakota

Northern State University
http://www.northern.edu

South Dakota School of Mines and
Technology
http://www.sdsmt.edu

South Dakota State University
http://www.sdstate.edu

University of South Dakota
http://www.usd.edu

190

Tennessee

Belmont University
http://www.belmont.edu

Carson-Newman College
http://www.cn.edu

Freed-Hardeman University
http://www.fhu.edu

Lincoln Memorial University
http://www.lmunet.edu

Union University
http://www.uu.edu

University of Memphis
http://www.memphis.edu

University of Tennessee
http://www.tennessee.edu

University of Tennessee—Chattanooga
http://www.utc.edu

University of Tennessee—Martin
http://www.utm.edu

University of the South
http://www.sewanee.edu

Vanderbilt University
http://www.vanderbilt.edu

Texas

Baylor University
http://www.baylor.edu

Midwestern State University
http://www.mwsu.edu

Rice University
http://www.rice.edu

Saint Mary's University
http://www.stmarytx.edu

St. Edward's University
http://www.stedwards.edu

Stephen F. Austin State University
http://www.sfasu.edu

Sul Ross State University
http://www.sulross.edu

Texas A&M University
http://www.tamu.edu

Texas Tech University
http://www.ttu.edu

University of Dallas
http://www.udallas.edu

University of Houston
http://www.uh.edu

University of North Texas
http://www.unt.edu

University of Texas
http://www.utsystem.edu

Utah

Brigham Young University
http://www.byu.edu/home2.html

Southern Utah University
http://www.suu.edu

University of Utah
http://www.utah.edu

Utah State University
http://www.usu.edu

Vermont

Bennington College
http://www.bennington.edu

Middlebury College
http://www.middlebury.edu/

Norwich University
http://www.norwich.edu

University of Vermont
http://www.uvm.edu

Virginia

College of William and Mary
http://www.wm.edu

George Mason University
http://www.gmu.edu

Hampton University
http://www.hamptonu.edu

James Madison University
http://www.jmu.edu

Liberty University
http://www.liberty.edu

Marymount University
http://www.marymount.edu

Old Dominion University
http://www.odu.edu

Radford University
http://www.radford.edu

University of Richmond
http://www.Richmond.edu

Virginia (cont.)

University of Virginia
http://www.Virginia.EDU

Virginia Intermont College
http://www.vic.edu

Washington and Lee University
http://www.wlu.edu

Washington

Eastern Washington University
http://www.ewu.edu

Pacific Lutheran University
http://www.plu.edu

Seattle Pacific University
http://www.spu.edu

Seattle University
http://www.seattleu.edu

University of Washington
http://www.washington.edu

Washington State University
http://www.wsu.edu

West Virginia

Shepherd College
http://www.shepherd.edu

University of Charleston
http://www.uchaswv.edu

West Virginia University
http://www.wvu.edu

West Virginia University Institute of
Technology
http://www.wvit.wvnet.edu

West Virginia Wesleyan College
http://www.wvwc.edu

Wisconsin

Lawrence University
http://www.lawrence.edu

Marquette University
http://www.Marquette.edu

Milwaukee School of Engineering
http://www.msoe.edu

Saint Norbert College
http://www.snc.edu

University of Wisconsin—Madison
http://www.wisc.edu

University of Wisconsin—Superior
http://www.uwsuper.edu

Wyoming

University of Wyoming
http://www.uwyo.edu

Kaplan International Locations

You can find Kaplan centers in various countries outside the United States for test preparation and admissions consulting. Our centers outside the United States offer test preparation for the SAT, GMAT, GRE, USMLE, TOEFL, and much more. Best of luck with your studies!

CANADA

Montreal Center
Kaplan Educational Center
550 Sherbrooke West, Suite 550
Montreal, Quebec H3A 1BP
Canada
P: (514) 287-1896
F: (514) 287-1292
E: anges_carrara@kaplan.com
W: www.kaptest.com

Toronto Center
Kaplan Educational Center
180 Bloor Street West, 4th Floor
Toronto, Ontario M5S 2V6
Canada
P: (416) 967-4733
F: (416) 967-0771
E: fiona_haldane@kaplan.com
W: www.kaptest.com

Vancouver Center
Kaplan Educational Center
1490 West Broadway Avenue
Third Floor, Vancouver, BC V6H
1H5 Canada
P: (604) 734-8378
F: (604) 734-8883
E: bill_osborne@kaplan.com
W: www.kaptest.com

CHINA

Hong Kong Center
Scholastic Bridges/Kaplan
Educational Center
1/FL ChiWo Commercial Bldg.
20 Saigon Street, Kowloon
Hong Kong
P: (852) 2359-9033
F: (852) 2359-9100
E: info@kaplan.com.hk
W: www.kaplan.com.hk

COLOMBIA

Bogota Center
Test Prep Center E.U./
Kaplan Educational Center
Calle 93A No. 10-55
Bogota, Colombia
P: (571) 257-7311
F: (571) 257-8624
E: colombia@kaplan.com
W: www.kaplan.com.co

EGYPT

Alexandria Center
Middle East Continuing
Education & Training Center/
Kaplan Educational Center
20 Sorya Street, Roshdi
Alexandria, Egypt
P/F: (2-03) 545-5747
E: ckaplan@link.com.eg

Cairo Center
Middle East Continuing
Education & Training Center/
Kaplan Educational Center
31 El Hegas Street, Heliopolise
Cairo, Egypt
P/F: (2-02) 450-2142
E: ckaplan@link.com.eg

Mansourah Center
Middle East Continuing
Education & Training Center/
Kaplan Educational Center
Al-Gomhoriya Street
Mansourah, Egypt
P/F: (2-05) 036-0885
E: ckaplan@link.com.eg

FRANCE

Paris Center
Kaplan Educational Center
3 bix rue Alex Carrel
75015 Paris, France
P: (33-1) 4566-5533
F: (33-1) 4566-0840
E: paris_center@kaplan.com
W: www.kaptest.com

INDIA

Main Office/Hyderabad Center
Indo-American Industries/
Kaplan Educational Center
602 & 603 Paigah Plaza
Basheer Bagh, Hyderabad
500229, India
P: (91-40) 329-6400
F: (91-40) 323-0475
E: iapen@hd1.vsnl.net.in

Bangalore Center
Indo-American Industries/
Kaplan Educational Center
192, First Floor, Sankey Road
Sadashivnagar, Bangalore 60080
India
P: (91-80) 331-1825
F: (91-80) 346-2306
E: iapen@vsnl.com

Chennai Center
Indo-American Industries/
Kaplan Educational Center
No. 94, New Awadi Road
(Opposite Pachappa College)
Kilpauk, Chennai 600010, India
P: (91-44) 642-9889
F: n/a
E: iapen@vsnl.com

Mumbai Center
EPCA Ltd./ Kaplan Educational
Center
Mumbai Education Trust
Building
First Floor, Opp. Leelavathi
Hospital, Bandra Reclamation
Mumbai 400050, India
P: (91-22) 651-6200
F: n/a
E: epca@hotmail.com

New Delhi Center
Indo-American Industries/
Kaplan Educational Center
M-11, Green Park (Main)
New Delhi 110016, India
P: (91-11) 651-3855
F: n/a
E: iapen@email.com

JAPAN

Tokyo Center-Aoyama
Eikoh/Kaplan Educational
Center
Sogetsu-Kaikan, 8th Floor
7-2-21 Akasaka, Minato-Ku
Tokyo 107-0052, Japan
P: (81-3) 3403-3546
F: (81-3) 3403-3547
E: kap-info@kaplan.ac.jp
W: www.kaplan.ac.jp

Tokyo Center-Ginza
Eikoh/ Kaplan Educational
Center
Namiki Building, 3rd Floor
3-2-10 Ginza Chuo,
Tokyo 104-0061, Japan
P: (81-3) 3538-4983
F: (81-3) 3538-4984
E: kap-info@kaplan.ac.jp
W: www.kaplan.ac.jp

(continued)

Kaplan International Locations
JAPAN (cont.)
Nagoya Center
Gakuyu Shuppan Company
Limited/Kaplan Educational
Center
Proto Shinsakae Bldg.
5th Floor
1-8-35 Shinsakae Naka-ku
Nagoya, Aichi 460-0007, Japan
P: (81-52) 252-0020
F: (81-52) 263-5673
E: kaplan-nagoya@aozora.com
W: www.kaplan.ac.jp

KOREA
Seoul Center
J EduLine/Kaplan Educational
Center
Shingu Building,
620-2 Shinsa-dong, Kangnam-ku
Seoul, 135-280, Korea
P: (82-2) 3444-1230
F: (82-2) 517-1230
E: ochoo@joins.com
W: www.kaplankorea.com

PANAMA
Panama City Center
Edutech, Inc./ Kaplan
Educational Center
Calle de CrediCorp Bank
Entre Calle 50 y Israel
Box 55-2706, Paitilla
Panama City, Panama
P: (507) 223-5445
F: (507) 223-5443
E: edutech@pty.com

PHILIPPINES
Makati City Center
International Cultural Studies
and Education Corporation
(ICSEC)/Kaplan Educational
Center
Unit 113, Ground Floor
Anson Arcade
167 Arnaiz Avenue
(formerly Pasay Road)
Makati City, Philippines
P: (63-2) 813-8222
P: (63-2) 813-8282
F: (63-2) 817-8787
E: kaplan.mkt@lkg.com.ph

Quezon City Center
International Cultural Studies
and Education Corporation
(ICSEC)/Kaplan Educational
Center
3rd Floor Z Executive Suites
1132 Quezon Avenue
Quezon City, Philippines
P: (63-2) 371-8966
P: (63-2) 371-8968
F: (63-2) 371-8967
E: kaplan.qc@lkg.com.ph

Cebu City Center
International Cultural Studies
and Education Corporation
(ICSEC)/Kaplan Educational
Center
Winland Tower Condominium
Juana Osmena Extension
Room 709
(Room 1607-1608 after 5pm)
Cebu City, Philippines
P: (63-32) 412-9977
F: (63-32) 412-9964
E: kaplan.cebu@lkg.com.ph

POLAND
Main Office/ Katowice Center
American Academy of English
Sp. z o.o./Kaplan Educational
Center
ul. Slowackiego 16
40-094 Katowice, Poland
P/F: (48-32) 253-0272
E: info@ameracad.com
W: www.ameracad.com

Bytom Center
American Academy of English
Sp. z o.o./ Kaplan Educational
Center
ul. Sadowa 5
41-902 Bytom, Poland
P: (48-32) 281-3522
F: (48-32) 281-3629
E: info@ameracad.com
W: www.ameracad.com

Czestochowa Center
American Academy of English
Sp. z o.o./Kaplan Educational
Center
al. NMP 17
42-200 Czestochowa, Poland
P: (48-34) 361-1632
F: (48-34) 361-1233
E: info@ameracad.com
W: www.ameracad.com

Gliwice Center
American Academy of English
Sp. z o.o./ Kaplan Educational
Center
ul. Zwyciestwa 14
44-100 Gliwice, Poland
P: (48-32) 238-9697
F: (48-32) 238-9336
E: info@ameracad.com
W: www.ameracad.com

Lodz Center
American Academy of English
Sp. z o.o./Kaplan Educational
Center
ul. Wolnosci 12
91-415 Lodz, Poland
P/F: (48-42) 639-8064
E: info@ameracad.com
W: www.ameracad.com

Opole Center
American Academy of English
Sp. z o.o./Kaplan Educational
Center
ul. Damrota 10
45-064 Opole, Poland
P: (48-77) 453-9384
F: (48-77) 453-9557
E: info@ameracad.com
W: www.ameracad.com

Sosnowiec Center
American Academy of English
Sp. z o.o./Kaplan Educational
Center
ul. 3 Maja 30
41-200 Sosnowiec, Poland
P: (48-32) 785-0290
F: (48-32) 266-4477
E: info@ameracad.com
W: www.ameracad.com

Warsaw Center
American Academy of English
Sp. z o.o./Kaplan Educational
Center
ul. Nowy Swiat 54/56
00-042 Warsaw, Poland
P: (48-22) 826-2465
F: (48-22) 826-8859
E: info@ameracad.com
W: www.ameracad.com

Wroclaw Center
American Academy of English
Sp. z o.o./Kaplan Educational
Center
ul. Kazimierza Wielkiego 27
50-077 Wroclaw, Poland
P: (48-71) 341-7746
F: (48-71) 341-7587
E: info@ameracad.com
W: www.ameracad.com

SAUDI ARABIA
Main Office/Jeddah Center
Middle East Continuing
Education & Training Center/
Kaplan Educational Center
New Jeddah Clinic Hospital
Palestine Square
Madina Road - PO Box 7692
Jeddah 21472, Saudi Arabia
P: (966-2) 667-5000
F: (966-2) 665-3332
E: jkaplan@zajil.net

Al-Khobar Center
Middle East Continuing
Education & Training Center/
Kaplan Educational Center
Prince Faisal Bin Fah'd Street
Al-Khobar, Eastern Region
Saudi Arabia
P: (966-3) 864-8644
F: (966-3) 864-9945
E: jkaplan@zajil.net

Riyadh Center- Al-Manahil
(Females Only)
Middle East Continuing
Education & Training Center/
Kaplan Educational Center
Al-Manahil, Diplomatic
Quarters
P.O. Box 61174, Riyadh, 11565
Saudi Arabia
P/F: (966-1) 488-1069 Ext. 209
E: jkaplan@zajil.net

Riyadh Center- Al-Sulimaniah
(Males & Females Welcome)
Middle East Continuing
Education & Training Center/
Kaplan Educational Center
Al-Sulimaniah- Thalathin Street
(In front of Al-Mustaqbal
Schools)
Riyadh, Saudi Arabia
P: (966-1) 462-7778
F: (966-1) 462-7778
E: jkaplan@zajil.net

SINGAPORE
Business Technology Institute
Ltd. Pte./Kaplan Educational
Center
135 Middle Road
#04-12/13 Bylands Building
Singapore 188975
P: (65) 336-2611
F: (65) 338-9864
E: alberton@pacific.net.sg

SPAIN
Madrid Center
Enforex/Kaplan Educational
Center
C/Baltasar Gracián, 4
28015 Madrid, Spain
P: (34-91) 547-2539
F: (34-91) 594-5159
E: kaplan@enforex.es
W: www.enforex.com

THAILAND
Bangkok Center
Star EDU Co., Ltd./ Kaplan
Educational Center
5th Floor, Bangkok Bank
Building
394 Siam Square Soi 5
Rama 1 Road, Pathumwan
Bangkok 10330, Thailand
P: (662) 658-3991
F: (662) 658-4354
E: kaplan@anet.net.th

TURKEY
Istanbul Center
Pen Academies/ Kaplan
Educational Center
Buyukdere Caddesi Hurhan 15/A
80260 Sisli, Istanbul, Turkey
P: (90-212) 225-7171
F: (90-212) 219-6509
E: kaplan_turkey@kaplan.com

UNITED KINGDOM
London Center
Kaplan Educational Center
3-5 Charing Cross Road
London WC2H 0HA England
P: (44-20) 7930-3130
F: (44-20) 7930-8009
E: london_center@kaplan.com
W: www.kaptest.com

VENEZUELA
Caracas Center
US Test Prep S.A./
Kaplan Educational Center
Avenida Francisco de Miranda
Urbanización Los Palos Grandes
Local No. LCC2 - 13
Edificio Parque Cristal, Caracas
Venezuela
P: (58-14) 248-0349
P: (58-14) 248-0394
E: venezuela@kaplan.com.co
W: www.kaplan.com.ve

Need more information about Kaplan centers outside the US? Contact us!

Office of Licensee Operations/
Kaplan International
370 Seventh Avenue
Suite 306
New York, NY 10001 USA
P: 917.339.7597
F: 917.339.7505
E: licensee_operations@kaplan.com